Texas-Style Exclusion

Texas-Style Exclusion

Mexican Americans and the Legacy of Limited Opportunity

Jennifer Van Hook and James D. Bachmeier

Russell Sage Foundation ~ New York

The Russell Sage Foundation

The Russell Sage Foundation, one of the oldest of America's general purpose foundations, was established in 1907 by Mrs. Margaret Olivia Sage for "the improvement of social and living conditions in the United States." The foundation seeks to fulfill this mandate by fostering the development and dissemination of knowledge about the country's political, social, and economic problems. While the foundation endeavors to assure the accuracy and objectivity of each book it publishes, the conclusions and interpretations in Russell Sage Foundation publications are those of the authors and not of the foundation, its trustees, or its staff. Publication by Russell Sage, therefore, does not imply foundation endorsement.

ROR: https://ror.org/02yh9se80
DOI: https://doi.org/10.7758/fhka5464

Library of Congress Cataloging-in-Publication Data

Names: Van Hook, Jennifer, author. | Bachmeier, James D., author.
Title: Texas-style exclusion : Mexican Americans and the legacy of limited opportunity / Jennifer Van Hook and James D. Bachmeier.
Description: New York : Russell Sage Foundation, [2024] | Includes bibliographical references and index. | Summary: "Texas-Style Exclusion shows that Mexican immigrants, the nation's largest contemporary immigrant group, encountered an inhospitable environment when they started settling in Texas in the early twentieth century. It was far more repressive and offered far fewer opportunities than those provided to the millions of children of immigrants living in the Northeast and Midwest. Moreover, the initial disadvantages for Mexican immigrants living in Texas in the 1920s and 1930s were transmitted to their children, and to some extent their grandchildren, leading to their slow rates of upward mobility and social integration. The authors focus especially on educational attainment since it is a major indicator of a group's socioeconomic position in the United States. Educational attainment is strongly related to a person's access to schooling and is a crucial predictor of other important life outcomes, including income, occupation, health, and even length of life. Unlike other indicators of immigrant integration such as income, occupation, or residential segregation, education is easily interpretable and is measured consistently across all the census data sources examined"—Provided by publisher.
Identifiers: LCCN 2024027125 (print) | LCCN 2024027126 (ebook) | ISBN 9780871548573 (paperback) | ISBN 9781610449298 (ebook)
Subjects: LCSH: Mexican Americans—Texas—Social conditions. | Mexican Americans—Texas—Economic conditions. | Race discrimination—Texas. | Educational attainment—Texas. | Social mobility—Texas.
Classification: LCC F395.M5 V36 2024 (print) | LCC F395.M5 (ebook) | DDC 305.868/720730764—dc23/eng/20240807
LC record available at https://lccn.loc.gov/2024027125
LC ebook record available at https://lccn.loc.gov/2024027126

Text design by Genna Patacsil. Front matter DOI: https://doi.org/10.7758/fhka5464.2774

RUSSELL SAGE FOUNDATION
112 East 64th Street, New York, New York 10065
10 9 8 7 6 5 4 3 2 1

In memory of George and Grace Mulder

~ Contents ~

~ Illustrations ~

Figures

Photos

Tables

Additional material can be found in the online supplement at https://www.russellsage.org/publications/texas-style-exclusion.

~ About the Authors ~

Jennifer Van Hook ⓘ is Distinguished Professor of Sociology and Demography at the Pennsylvania State University.

James D. Bachmeier ⓘ is associate professor of sociology at Temple University.

~ Preface~

I grew interested in immigrant integration by observing the responses to immigrants arriving today of many Americans who are themselves descendants of earlier generations of immigrants. I grew up in Holland, Michigan, a community in western Michigan that was essentially a Dutch immigrant enclave. Most of the people who lived there had Dutch last names (such as names starting with "Van" or "De") and could trace their ancestry to immigrants who arrived from the Netherlands between about 1860 and 1920. The city regularly celebrated its ethnic heritage at its annual "Tulip Time" festival. The high school marching band wore wooden shoes. Even though many of the original Dutch immigrants were poor and uneducated, those memories were long gone. When I was growing up in Holland, there was tremendous pride in being Dutch, and the closer a person's connection to the Netherlands—via travel, ancestry, food, or use of the Dutch language—the better.

In the 1970s and 1980s, however, Holland started to become a new destination for Mexican immigrants, many of whom traveled north to work in the area's fruit and manufacturing industries. Some of the poorest children in my school were the children of these Mexican workers. Today about half of the city's schoolchildren are Hispanic. Although poverty rates are still high among the new immigrants, Holland has a growing Hispanic middle class. Some of the Hispanic friends I made growing up are now business owners, teachers, and college professors.

It has been a difficult transition for the community. Although efforts have been made to provide high-quality education and social services to the new immigrant families, there has been "white flight" from the area. Many white middle- and upper-class families moved out of the city to adjacent areas where the schools have fewer Hispanic students. There also has been political backlash. Western Michigan, long a politically conservative area, is now a stronghold of the MAGA movement. In an evolving story that made national news, a conservative group took over the governing board of the county in response to masking requirements during the COVID-19 pandemic. One of the new board's first actions was to change the motto of the county from "Where You Belong" to "Where Freedom Rings." It is as if they have forgotten the welcome and tolerance their Dutch ancestors once received as poor, non-English-speaking immigrants who were slow to "give up their foreign ways" over a century earlier.

My main goal in writing this book is to help readers see that all newcomers—regardless of where they came from or when they arrived in the United States—need a fair shot to be successful. This was true for the European immigrants who arrived over a century ago, and it is true for the Mexican immigrants who have arrived in the last few decades.

—Jenny Van Hook

Growing up in 1980s North Dakota, I encountered few immigrants. Our names—Anderson, Knudson, Nelson, and Nygaard; Braun, Schaefer, Schumacher, and Zimmerman—were legacies of the immigration experiences of our grandparents, but none of us thought of ourselves as immigrants. Ethnic identity was not a prominent axis of social organization in my childhood. The few remaining cultural markers of the immigrants did not factor prominently in our daily lives. Those of us from German-speaking backgrounds were raised Catholic and ate pierogi and *fleischkuekle* on special occasions, while my Scandinavian friends were more likely to attend Lutheran churches and eat things like lefse and lutefisk on special holidays. To the extent that my adolescent friends and I discussed it, we mostly thought of our immigrant origins as backward remnants of the past at ideological odds with our American futures.

We were all just American kids of the Cold War era. Whether true or not, a point of collective pride (and source of dread) in my youth was the assumption that, if we went to war with the Soviet Union, our town would be the second American site nuked, owing to the Strategic Air Command base located ten miles to the north. Our collective American experience and identity was strikingly uniform. We were all white, hailed from the same economic stratum (somewhere between working- and middle-class), and had been exposed to little of the abject poverty that was prevalent on the state's five Native reservations. We all went to well-resourced schools and received rigorous educations that prepared us for postsecondary opportunities, which were plentiful.

What I didn't fully realize growing up was that I represented the late stages of a classical American assimilation story. I knew—because I was told—that we had what we had in life because of hard work, thanks to a work ethic that was handed down by immigrant, homesteading grandparents and great-grandparents. What I didn't realize then was the part of my story that we try to tell in this book: all of my family's hard work would have meant little if we had not been afforded opportunities along the way.

My story, and the story that we tell in this book, is ultimately a story of investment. Alongside other large-scale Industrial Era investments in the nation's infrastructure, the social safety net, and homeownership, a massive expansion in public school investments helped launch millions of children of European immigrants onto a rocketlike trajectory of upward mobility. These opportunities were not afforded to most non-Europeans of the Industrial Era, and the resulting inequality has been with us to this day. To the extent that such systematic inequality contradicts our fundamental national ideals, I believe it is crucial to thoroughly understand how systematic exclusion operated in the past so that we can work to ameliorate it in the present and future. My hope is that this book will contribute to that understanding.

—James Bachmeier

~ Acknowledgments ~

This book was written with the support of the Russell Sage Foundation, which provided generous funding for the project (G-6619) and our sabbatical leaves as visiting scholars at its headquarters in New York City (G-1904-14380, G-1906-16952). Other RSF visiting scholars provided helpful feedback on the project in its early stages of development. We are particularly grateful for the comments we received from Marta Tienda. In addition to helping us think about access to higher education, she shared her own life story and told us about the opportunities she and her siblings had when her family moved from Texas to Michigan when she was a child. The RSF staff were instrumental in the production of the book, including RSF director of publications Suzanne Nichols. Our editor, Alison Ward of The Editing Ward, improved the readability and arguments of the book, making it accessible to a broader set of readers beyond our academic peers. We also want to thank our graduate student assistants: Kendal Lowrey helped create and manage the analysis of the linked census data, and Cheyenne Lonobile helped assemble, clean, and manage the Biennial Survey of Education (BSE) data. Three undergraduate students, Delaney Greczyn and Caroline Sene from Penn State University and Amira Solomon from Temple University, conducted data quality checks on the scanned BSE data. We also worked extensively with the U.S. Census Bureau staff throughout the project. We are particularly grateful for help provided by Brad Foster, Erik Vickstrom, Mark Leach, Katie Genadek, and Emily Greenman. Thank you also to Doug Oswald, marketing director of the American Seating Company, who took the time to answer our emails and share old issues of the company's magazine, *Seater*, about the company's efforts to integrate immigrant workers during the 1920s and 1930s; the archivists of the Grand Rapids History Center of the Grand Rapids Public Library, who helped locate the photos of Jenny's grandparents; and to Johnny Rodriguez, CEO of Latin Americans United for Progress (LAUP), who answered our emails about LAUP's work in western Michigan.

Finally, we are grateful for the support of our families. Jenny is especially appreciative of her husband Stephen and children Jacob and Dietre, who offered encouragement as she wrote the book; her mother, Judy, who shared family stories; and her Aunt Kathy, who found and sent us old work photos of her grandfather, George Mulder, from the archives of the American Seating Company's magazine. Jim is beyond grateful for the endless support of his spouse Jen, and daughter Kaia. He is also thankful for the support, family stories, photos, and genealogical research provided by his parents, Dean and Norma Bachmeier.

~ Chapter 1 ~

Digging into the Archives

In 1994, the General Social Survey asked people whether they agreed with the following statement: "The Irish, Italians, Jews, and many other minorities overcame prejudice and worked their way up. Today's immigrants should do the same without special favors."[1]

Four out of five respondents agreed with the statement. At that time, three-quarters of Americans were non-Hispanic white, and the majority had descended from the massive wave of Southern and Eastern Europeans received in the United States during the late nineteenth and early twentieth centuries.[2] Their belief that the Irish, Italians, and Jews could succeed without special favors likely reflects understandings of their own families' successes. After all, if their families did it on their own, new immigrants should too.

For Americans with European origins, family immigration stories typically start with an immigration journey, impoverished beginnings, and hard work, and they end with economic upward mobility and social integration. This was certainly the case for us, the authors of this book. Although of different ethnic origins, both of us grew up in a family in which immigration featured prominently in narratives about the family's success.

Jenny's family moved to western Michigan from the Netherlands during the late nineteenth and early twentieth centuries. Her mother's parents, Grace Oosting and George Mulder, worked diligently to overcome their impoverished origins (photos 1.1 and 1.2). Grace's family was so poor after her father died that they did not have enough money to buy appropriately sized shoes for her, leading to lifelong, debilitating foot problems. George's alcoholic father abandoned the family, prompting George to work at an early age to support his non-English-speaking mother. Despite coming from "broken" impoverished families, both Grace and George graduated

https://doi.org/10.7758/fhka5464.7487

Photo 1.1 *Grace Oosting, Jenny's Grandmother, Senior Photo, Union High School, Grand Rapids, Michigan, 1929*

GRACE LaVERNE OOSTING
Commercial Course. Birthday, June 11.
Attended Widdicomb School. Member
of Harrison High-lights Staff, Memorial
Committee, Service Squad, President
of Audubon Club, Vice-President of
Girl Reserves.
An unfailing good-humor endears her to many.

Source: Courtesy of the Grand Rapids History Center of the Grand Rapids Public Library.

from high school in the late 1920s, a time when only 29 percent of youth did so. George later worked his way up the ladder at American Seating, a furniture company in Grand Rapids, Michigan, and eventually served as a vice president. All four of their children attained an MD or PhD and worked as a professional in their field.

Jim's immigrant ancestors came from German-speaking communities that had settled in present-day Moldova and Ukraine in the late eighteenth century. Motivated in part by the opportunity to acquire farmland through the Homestead Act (1862), his great-grandparents settled in North Dakota communities of transplanted Germans from Russia during the first two

Photo 1.2 *George Mulder, Jenny's Grandfather, Featured in an Article about His Work at American Seating Company in Grand Rapids, Michigan*

George Mulder, the department's Chief Estimator, carefully studies blue prints and specifications for "X"; with co-workers, e s t i m a t e s costs. Cost department takes over, determines selling price, which is used by War Contracts Division for bidding.

Source: Seater, December 1943, courtesy of the Grand Rapids History Center of the Grand Rapids Public Library.

decades of the twentieth century, part of a patchwork mosaic of immigrants of mostly Northern and Western European nationalities who settled the state. Initially, homesteaders on the barren plains of North Dakota—a landscape that resembled the wheat fields of the Black Sea region in the "old country"—were probably more concerned with survival than with integration into their newly adopted country. For example, Jim's great-grandparents, Joseph and Otilla Bachmeier, were married in the village of Krasne (in present-day Ukraine) in 1892 and had four children there. Shortly after settling in southern North Dakota around 1906, all four children died from an unknown illness. The couple gave birth to six additional children in the United States, all of whom survived. They included Jim's grandfather, Peter Bachmeier, who was born in 1910 (photo 1.3).

The integration of the German-speaking Russian immigrants of North Dakota into American life was slow to nonexistent in the initial decades after settlement, owing most likely to a combination of factors, including the lack of infrastructure and institutions in the state, which only entered

Photo 1.3 *Jim's Grandparents, Peter and Ipprozina Bachmeier, 1932*

Source: Author's collection.

the union in 1889, and prairie isolation in small ethnically and linguistically homogeneous communities that were highly dependent on one another for survival. German-speaking households persisted for decades, including that of Jim's father; born in 1941, he grew up speaking mostly German at home as a child. Compulsory participation in the developing rural school system was often viewed in these communities as being at odds with the demand for children's labor on the family farm.[3] This attitude began to change after World War II with the development of towns and small cities in North Dakota that offered opportunities outside of farming. Jim's parents and their siblings all completed high school, and many went on to earn bachelor's and master's degrees and establish upwardly mobile non-agricultural careers in education, real estate, health care, and other burgeoning industries, both within the state and in other parts of the country. Reflecting a common Industrial Era immigration story, this upward and geographic mobility of German-Russians from North Dakota accelerated in the third and later generations—those born during the 1960s, '70s, and '80s—as access to postsecondary education became more widespread.[4] Many of Jim's siblings and cousins, now spread across the nation, attained college and postsecondary degrees leading to professional occupations and a place in the American middle class.

Stories such as these exemplify the American dream. They optimistically signal the capacity for the country to integrate immigrants, even those of very poor origins. They also undergird Americans' complex feelings about immigration. Right now, despite strong political polarization on the issue, support for legal immigration among Americans is high. According to polling conducted in 2018 by the Pew Research Center, in the middle of the Trump presidency, 70 percent of Americans favored either maintaining (38 percent) or increasing (32 percent) legal immigration levels beyond the three-quarters of a million or so admitted to the country every year.[5] However, Americans' fondness for immigration is conditional. Immigrants are welcome if they can make it on their own. For example, in a 2021 Cato Institute survey, 58 percent of respondents favored increasing immigration on the condition that immigrants proved that they would not use government assistance.[6]

The problem with the expectation that immigrants will be self-sufficient, however, is that it is based on incomplete and inaccurate memories. Most people suffer from a form of "temporal nearsightedness," that is, a blurry view of the past. When thinking about the events that occurred a century or more ago, they especially tend to forget about the help their families once received. When people think of support, they often think narrowly of welfare programs, like cash or food assistance. But support can take many different forms, including public schooling, the GI Bill, and loan programs to promote homeownership.

Jenny's grandparents, George and Grace, benefited from living in an urban area in Michigan with well-funded public schools.[7] Jenny recently browsed their high school yearbook, available from the Grand Rapids History Center of the Grand Rapids Public Library, and found that both Grace and George graduated with a specialized commercial high school degree. Their teachers were highly educated, with most having a bachelor's degree. Both participated in their school's clubs and extracurricular activities; Grace was active in the Audubon and service clubs, and George in the science club. George later obtained a certificate in drafting through a program paid for by the Grand Rapids Public School System. We looked up what schools were spending on instruction in that time: In 1930, Grand Rapids public schools spent $134 per pupil each year, nearly twice the national average of $72.[8]

Additionally, the company where George worked, American Seating, was strongly aligned with the Progressive movement, a religious and political movement that sought to improve education, work, and health conditions in the early twentieth century. Jenny learned about American Seating's involvement in the Progressive movement only after she visited the company and browsed through the archives of the company publication, *Seater*, a bimonthly journal that featured employee news (for example, births, marriages, and reports on company sports teams and the annual company picnic), articles about the company's products, management philosophy, and advice to workers. Originally known as the American School Furniture Company, the company manufactured children's desks for the country's rapidly expanding public school systems during the early twentieth century. The company saw itself as a modernizing force, transforming "backward" conditions in "primitive schools" (descriptors used in an article in *Seater*) into functional learning environments where all children could obtain an education regardless of where they lived or their family background.[9] American Seating also sought to improve the lives of its workers. In the early 1920s, about 25 percent of the workforce in Grand Rapids was foreign-born, and an additional 35 percent were U.S.-born children of immigrants.

To integrate its foreign-born employees (a process referred to at the time as "Americanization"), the company offered English language and civics classes to workers and regularly provided updates of the number and names of employees who had become naturalized U.S. citizens (photo 1.4).[10] The company also promoted individual self-improvement. To encourage workers to extend their education, it provided a company library. One article in *Seater* outlined a rigorous course of study for those seeking to educate themselves.[11] The company also encouraged workers to enroll in night school courses (photo 1.5) and summer educational programs and advocated against child labor.[12] Besides promoting health through improvements in workplace safety, the retention of a company nurse, and regular communications on topics like nutrition, sleep, and sanitation, it also encouraged workers to save money and buy homes. *Seater* frequently published photographs of employee homes purchased through its loan program. Finally, American Seating promoted higher education by recognizing workers' children who graduated from high school or who earned special school honors, such as being named a valedictorian or going on to college.

Even though Jenny's grandparents George and Grace grew up in poverty and their immigrant parents had very little education and knew little English, the public school system and the company where George worked provided a clear road map and resources for launching themselves and their children into the American middle class. Like many children of immigrants today, George and Grace worked hard, but in their case hard work paid off because the environment they lived in provided opportunities for upward mobility. Details about these opportunities were missing from the stories Jenny heard when growing up. Being temporally nearsighted (like most people), she was unaware of the resources to which her grandparents had access until she dug into the history of the institutions where they studied and worked. The resources available to George and Grace were not discussed much in family stories, yet they were clearly evident in the archives of the Grand Rapids public school yearbooks and issues of *Seater*.

Though the details vary, the immigrant story Jim came to know growing up similarly stressed the importance of hard work, self-reliance, and perse-

Photo 1.4 *"Americanization"*

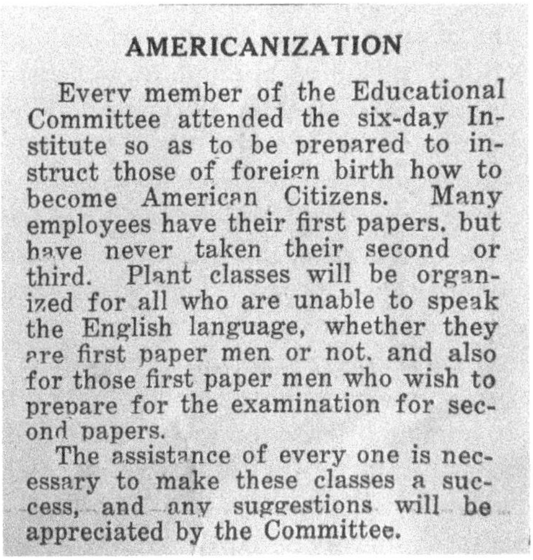

AMERICANIZATION

Every member of the Educational Committee attended the six-day Institute so as to be prepared to instruct those of foreign birth how to become American Citizens. Many employees have their first papers, but have never taken their second or third. Plant classes will be organized for all who are unable to speak the English language, whether they are first paper men or not, and also for those first paper men who wish to prepare for the examination for second papers.

The assistance of every one is necessary to make these classes a success, and any suggestions will be appreciated by the Committee.

Source: American Seating Company, 1919. Reprinted with permission.
Note: Citizenship and English classes were offered to employees at
the American Seating Company, Grand Rapids, Michigan.

Photo 1.5 *"Night Schools"*

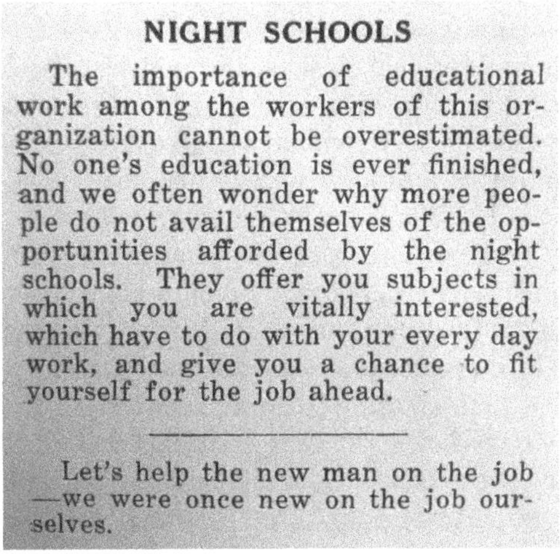

NIGHT SCHOOLS

The importance of educational work among the workers of this organization cannot be overestimated. No one's education is ever finished, and we often wonder why more people do not avail themselves of the opportunities afforded by the night schools. They offer you subjects in which you are vitally interested, which have to do with your every day work, and give you a chance to fit yourself for the job ahead.

Let's help the new man on the job —we were once new on the job ourselves.

Source: American Seating Company, 1922. Reprinted with permission.
Note: American Seating encouraged its employees to extend their education by
taking night school classes, which were offered by the Grand Rapids Public
Schools, and reminded its workers to help new employees.

verance in forging a life on the windswept plains of North Dakota. Less emphasized were the government and institutional supports that developed to create a structure of opportunities for upward mobility and the incentives, for all Americans, including immigrants and their descendants, to pursue them: the granting of free land through the Homestead Act; the subsequent development of a progressive school system to provide for the education of the immigrant homesteaders' children; the development of a higher education system providing low-cost access to postsecondary schooling; and myriad federal programs and investments that fueled the post–World War II modernization of the rural Upper Midwest, such as electrification and the interstate highway system.

Besides leading people to forget about the help their families once received, temporal nearsightedness leads people to have unrealistic expectations for today's immigrants. Television journalist Tom Brokaw displayed such nearsightedness on NBC's *Meet the Press* in 2019 when he reiterated his long-held view that "Hispanics should work harder at assimilation." By saying that Hispanics should work harder, he was attributing their slow rates of integration to an unwillingness to do what was necessary to succeed, rather than to the unique challenges this group had faced. He also failed to distinguish Hispanics by the length of time they and their families had spent in the country. This is problematic because many Hispanic immigrants arrive as low-skill new arrivals, but their children and grandchildren tend to have more education and to work in higher-skilled jobs. Today half of Hispanic adults are immigrants, but Hispanic adults in the future are likely to have more education and lower rates of poverty as the immigrant generation passes away and is replaced by their U.S.-born children and grandchildren. Although Brokaw was widely criticized for his statement, and he issued an immediate apology, polls of people's concerns about immigrants suggest that his viewpoint still resonates widely.

Another example of temporal nearsightedness comes from Geno's, a landmark cheesesteak restaurant in South Philadelphia. The restaurant, founded by Joey Vento, a third-generation Italian American, found itself at the center of controversy in 2006 when Vento placed a sign in the restaurant's front window reading: THIS IS AMERICA: WHEN ORDERING PLEASE SPEAK ENGLISH. In news stories, Vento expressed that he was motivated to hang the sign by the increasing presence of Mexican immigrants in the neighborhood, which during the Industrial Era was Philadelphia's primary settlement enclave for the city's large population of poor Italian immigrants (Joey Vento's grandparents). Joey Vento passed away in 2011, but the sign remained in place until 2016, when it was finally removed.[13] Thus, the sign stood for a decade as a symbol—in a neighborhood steeped in immigration history—of the suspicions of previous waves of immigrants that new immigrants were not integrating into American life the "right way," seemingly oblivious to the fact that Joey Vento's Italian immigrant grandparents were greeted with similar suspicions by U.S. natives a century earlier.

What Tom Brokaw, Joey Vento, and others have overlooked, and what we show in this book, is that Mexican immigrants, the nation's largest contemporary immigrant group, encountered an inhospitable environment when they started settling in Texas in the early twentieth century. It was far more repressive and offered far fewer opportunities than the communities that welcomed George and Grace Mulder in Michigan, the offspring of Joseph and Otilla Bachmeier in North Dakota, Joey Vento's grandparents and the millions of other children of immigrants living in the Northeast and Midwest. Moreover, the initial disadvantages for Mexican immigrants living in Texas in the 1920s and 1930s were transmitted to their children and to some extent their grandchildren, leading to slow rates of upward mobility and social integration.

Temporal nearsightedness distorts our understanding of long-standing racial and ethnic inequalities and dampens our interest in supporting immigrants today. Gaining a more accurate picture of contemporary inequalities requires digging into the archives and filling in the gaps in our collective memories to recognize the historical conditions that helped European-origin immigrants and their offspring but hindered others. This is the primary goal of this book.

Mexican Americans as a Bellwether

Immigrant integration is vital for the social cohesion of the United States (or any national society that receives large numbers of immigrants). By integration, we are not talking about the cultural changes that typically occur when immigrants spend time in the host society. Rather, we are thinking more about the extent to which immigrants are accepted into the "organizations, institutional activities, and general civic life of the receiving society," to quote sociologist Milton Gordon.[14] The United States differs from many other nations in that its population is made up of a mixture of immigrant groups from a wide variety of national origins. Nearly all Americans, with the exception of indigenous persons and the descendants of slaves, whose migration was of course involuntary, can locate their American roots in one of the successive waves of immigration that have populated the nation over the last two and a half centuries. This includes the massive waves of immigrants who arrived during the Industrial Era between 1880 and 1924 and those who arrived during the current "post-1965" wave initiated by the passage of the 1965 Immigration and Nationality Act. The country has been able to maintain its unity because of an adherence to principles of equality, whereby all people share a common set of rights and responsibilities under its system of laws. Some of the darkest and most divisive periods in the United States have occurred when the nation failed to live up to this ideal.

Yet, despite their shared immigrant origins, the longer-settled American population has viewed subsequent waves of immigration with ambivalence. While immigration represents core elements of the American ideal and the engine of American nation-building, it also leads to social and demographic changes that raise concerns, both among social scientists and in the broader public, about the impact of immigration, and the seemingly bewildering cultural diversity it produces, on social cohesion in American life.[15]

These concerns, whether expressed in the theories of social scientists or in public opinion, betray doubt over whether the assimilation of immigrants will play out during the contemporary period of mass immigration in the same way that it is purported to have done in the past. Social scientists debate whether the children of today's immigrants will display the same rapid upward mobility and assimilation that characterized the American experiences of the children of poor European immigrants during the Industrial Era. For example, in his 2005 book *Italians Then, Mexicans Now*, economist Joel Perlmann draws parallels between the labor migrants of the Industrial Era (Italians) and those of today (Mexicans) and asks whether Mexican Americans will eventually follow the same path to the middle class taken by Italian Americans.[16] At the time he wrote his book, however, Perlmann was unable to follow immigrants and their descendants across generations, so his findings were inconclusive. Social scientists are therefore still asking: Will today's immigrant groups be integrated as equals into American society in a manner similar to the integration of Industrial Era European immigrant ethnic groups? Or will some of them instead be incorporated as impoverished racial groups?

Answering these questions requires us to reexamine (and sometimes correct) our collective memories of the past, so we can identify the factors that contributed to the apparent success of European immigrant groups and assess how conditions have changed since their era. Historians have provided rich and comprehensive descriptions of the experiences of immigrant families from multiple national origins, time periods, and places. Still, it is sometimes necessary to take a few steps back to see the overarching trends and patterns formed by this mosaic of historical information. Using the theory and methods of sociology and demography with the research conducted by historians, we were able to deduce the broad patterns of immigrant integration across the twentieth century.

We focused our efforts on outcomes for Mexican Americans relative to those of European-origin immigrants, specifically examining how educational attainment changed across generations—that is, from the first generation (immigrants) to the second generation (immigrants' U.S.-born children) and finally to the third generation (immigrants' grandchildren).

Mexican Americans constitute an important group warranting our attention in part because of the size of the group. The United States admits more immigrants from Mexico each year than from any other country, and in 2022 approximately 37.4 million Americans (11 percent of the U.S. population) identified as Mexican-origin. America's future competitiveness will depend on its ability to integrate Mexican immigrants and their descendants into a highly skilled workforce. This national concern is all the more pressing in light of the aging and low fertility of the U.S. population.[17]

Additionally, social scientists have positioned Mexican Americans as a test case, in the hope that the experiences of the descendants of Mexican immigrants may serve as a valid bellwether of contemporary integration dynamics.[18] As reflected in the title of Perlman's book *Italians Then, Mexicans Now*, Mexican immigrants are presumed to share a number of characteristics with Industrial Era European immigrants, whose "assimilability" was viewed with uncertainty and doubt among elites a century ago.[19] If the children of this generation's quintessential labor migrants—Mexicans—can rapidly climb the ladder into the middle class in a similar fashion as the offspring of Industrial Era labor migrants (Italians), that will provide evidence that the nation's opportunity structure is accessible to the descendants of immigrants with limited amounts of education and other resources. In many ways, Mexican Americans are key to answering fundamental questions about whether Industrial Era–style immigrant success stories are still possible on a large scale in present-day America.

In fact, the empirical evidence accumulated to date has led to a rather unsatisfying answer to the question of whether Mexican Americans are experiencing integration into American society as an upwardly mobile ethnic group or as a marginalized racial group. Somewhat paradoxically, the body of evidence points to the conclusion that Mexican Americans are experiencing both types of integration *simultaneously*.

Research on Mexican American integration has disproportionately relied on cross-sectional data, which are collected at a single point in time, as opposed to longitudinal data, which follow individuals and families over time. Studies that rely on cross-sectional data paint the most pessimistic picture. These studies present contemporary evidence of Mexican Americans' persistent disadvantage by comparing average levels of educational attainment across immigrant generations. When comparing education completion levels for different generational groups, it is common to observe a pattern of "third-generation delay" in which the educational attainment of Mexican Americans follows a nonlinear pattern across generations. The first generation (immigrants) has lower educational attainment than the second generation (U.S.-born children with at least one immigrant parent), but the third or higher generation (U.S.-born children with no immigrant parents) has similar or lower attainment than the second generation, and much lower attainment than non-Hispanic, U.S.-born whites.[20] This basic pattern of delay has been found in nearly every study of Mexican Americans using cross-sectional data from the U.S. Census Bureau.

Evidence of third-generation delay has been used to support arguments that contemporary assimilation has stalled.[21] It has even been used to argue that Mexican Americans are undergoing a process known as "downward assimilation." For example, in their highly influential paper, Alejandro Portes and Min Zhou predicted in 1993 that large numbers of the children of poor non-European immigrants would experience downward assimilation into a life of poverty and the attendant social dislocations disproportionately experienced by inner-city blacks.[22] They concluded that racial-minority immigrants such as Mexican Americans were likely to be incorporated into American society as a permanently disadvantaged racial group, part of a "rainbow underclass."

Studies based on other sources of cross-sectional data, however, offer more optimistic interpretations. Based on a sample of Mexican American adults in Los Angeles in 2004, Frank Bean, Susan Brown, and James Bachmeier present evidence of slow but steady upward mobility in their book *Parents without Papers*. They observe a pattern of educational progress across generations and argue that Mexican Americans' lower class position is temporary because it is strongly linked to the difficulties and challenges of living and working in the United States with unauthorized immigration status.[23] A large share of Mexican immigrants lack legal immigration status; without it, their opportunities in the labor market are curtailed and opportunities for their second-generation children are reduced. There is an argument to be made that these challenges are likely to fade for later generations, who will be U.S. citizens with U.S.-born parents. Cross-sectional data are nevertheless limited by the fact that they provide a snapshot of immigrant generations in the United States at a given point in time (or place) rather than following groups over time.[24]

Longitudinal data that follow individuals and families over time are better suited to the task of assessing intergenerational mobility because they are collected at multiple time points and can track changes for the same individuals or families. Influential studies based on longitudinal data, however, present a rather fragmented and incomplete assessment of Mexican American integration. On the one hand, in their recently published book *Streets of Gold*, economists Ran Abramitzky and Leah Boustan paint an optimistic picture of immigrant integration.[25] On the basis of their analysis of immigrants and their children, they report an uplifting story of immigrant mobility and success in which the children of immigrants of nearly every national origin group that arrived in the latter half of the twentieth century, including Mexicans, outperformed the children of U.S.-born parents. Exceeding expectations, the children of immigrants went further and did better in school and the labor market than their parents. Moreover, their rate of upward mobility outpaced the mobility seen among children with U.S.-born parents of similar socioeconomic backgrounds. However, Abramitzky and Boustan's data exclude Mexicans who arrived during the early decades of the twentieth century and therefore provide only a partial picture of Mexican immigrant integration, despite the fact that Mexican immigration to the United States spans more than a century.

On the other hand, sociologists Edward Telles and Vilma Ortiz are more pessimistic. In their 2008 book *Generations of Exclusion*, they employ data from a longitudinal survey that followed Mexican American families living in San Antonio and Los Angeles across three generations.[26] Like Abramitzky and Boustan, they find that most children of immigrants outperformed their parents, yet they also report them as remaining a lower-status group than U.S.-born, non-Hispanic whites, even after three generations of residence in the United States. However, the Telles and Ortiz longitudinal data represent a very different segment of the Mexican American population than the data employed by Abramitzky and Boustan. Specifically, the Telles and Ortiz sample includes the descendants of Mexican immigrants who arrived in the United States during the Industrial Era in two cities. Mexican Americans in Abramitzky and Boustan's analysis, by contrast, were more likely to be the descendants of Mexican immigrants who arrived in more recent decades. Thus, even existing longitudinal data can lead to inconsistent or contradictory findings when the temporal scope of the data differs across studies.

In this book, we use new longitudinal census data that are capable of presenting a more comprehensive assessment of Mexican American integration than has been possible until now. Surprisingly, our findings are consistent with both the optimistic and pessimistic perspectives. This might seem inexplicable, but the reason is quite simple: there has been significant variation in the opportunities available to Mexican Americans over time and across communities. Whether one is optimistic or pessimistic about the integration of Mexican Americans depends on *when* and *where* one looks.

As we discuss at greater length in chapter 2, recent innovations by the U.S. Census Bureau allow researchers to link individuals across historical censuses and survey data across decades.[27] We followed Industrial Era immigrant families over time, specifically from 1940, when immigrants were living in the United States with young children; to the 1970s and 1980s, when their children had established their own households; and finally to the present day, 2000 to 2021, when their grandchildren had reached adulthood. These new data linkages enabled us to piece together a picture of what happened to immigrant families over eight decades and across three generations. Additionally, because the data are national in scope, they encompass all the different places where Mexican Americans and other immigrants settled, not just individual cities like Los Angeles and San Antonio.

The focus of our study is educational attainment, an important indicator of a group's socioeconomic position in the United States. Educational attainment is strongly related to a person's access to schooling and is a crucial predictor of other important life outcomes, including income, occupation, health, and even length of life.[28] Unlike other indicators of immigrant integration, such as income, occupation, or residential segregation, education is easily interpretable and is measured consistently across all the census data sources we examine.

We combined the census data with historical archival data about the quality of public schooling in states and local areas across the nation during the Industrial Era. This newly digitized information about schools revealed tremendous regional variation in the educational opportunity available to children of immigrants across the United States in the early half of the twentieth century. Not all American children during the Industrial Era benefited from the same robust investments in schooling as the children of George and Grace Mulder and Joseph and Otilla Bachmeier in the Midwest.

The data revealed distinctive "vintages" within the Mexican American population. By "vintage" we refer to groups as defined by the period of history during which their ancestors first migrated to the United States. We adopt the term "vintage" rather than the commonly used demographic term "cohort" to signal two important points: First, the term moves us away from the idea that immigrant integration is an individual-level process. Cohorts are groups of *individuals* who were born in the same time period and who age together. In contrast, "vintages" are *families* who arrived in a given time period and can be followed across generations through time. Thus, the term "vintage" reminds us that an individual's challenges and successes are intertwined with those of their parents and grandparents. Second, we want to signal that integration is highly dependent on how immigrants are treated initially. Like aged wines whose quality depends on the combination of soil, temperature, and rainfall decades earlier, the educational attainment of the third generation depends on the past opportunities of their grandparents and parents. In this sense, the term "vintage" reminds us that historical inequality reverberates over time and can remain imprinted on the social structure decades later.

Our analyses of individual vintages revealed a substantial amount of variability in Mexican American mobility patterns. Older vintages were more likely to display patterns of intergenerational mobility in educational attainment that suggest their integration into American society as a marginalized racial group, roughly akin to the racial status of African Americans, even though Mexicans were considered white "by law" prior to the Civil Rights Era of the 1950s and 1960s. Third-generation delay is demonstrated in their descendants, today's third and fourth generations, which register particularly low levels of educational attainment in studies. In contrast, vintages with more recent origins, especially those beginning after the

Civil Rights Era (that is, after 1970), show patterns of intergenerational mobility in educational attainment that are more reminiscent of assimilation among European ethnic groups a century ago.

Furthermore, we find evidence among the earliest vintage of variation in mobility, specifically depending on whether one's immigrant ancestors lived in Texas, where the education system lagged behind non-Southern states in development. Before World War II, Mexican Americans in Texas were ensnared in an overtly racist Jim Crow institutional context that viewed them as a source of labor and upon whom investment in education would be wasted.[29] By contrast, California, the other hub of Industrial Era Mexican migration, had a far more developed school system and, like the urban school systems of the Northeast and Midwest, was heavily influenced by the Americanization movement. From today's vantage point, this social movement was ethnocentric; nevertheless, it sought in part to impress a unified national identity on the nation's mosaic of ethnoracial groups through the pursuit of education. Our data reveal an important source of heterogeneity that stems from the stark differences in early-vintage Mexican Americans' access to the expanding educational system, which varied dramatically depending on whether they lived in Texas, California, or other states.

Overview of the Book

In the following chapters, we tell the story, using our new data, of immigrant integration and Mexican American mobility over the course of the last century.

We begin in chapter 2 by laying out the significance of our investigation of Mexican American intergenerational mobility for ongoing debates about immigrant integration and the future of American society. We note the tendency for Mexican Americans to be viewed as a bellwether of contemporary integration, a test case that will resolve the seemingly intractable debates about immigration and the nation's changing color lines. In taking this view, however, researchers often have ignored or overlooked the fact that Mexican immigration dates back to the Industrial Era, which is most commonly associated with immigration from southern and eastern Europe. The long history of Mexican immigration to the United States has produced what we refer to as "vintage heterogeneity" in the Mexican American population. The later-generation (third, fourth, and beyond) Mexican Americans who are held up as indicators of contemporary assimilation descended from the earliest-arriving Mexican immigrant families. Their trajectories of intergenerational mobility were shaped by pre–Civil Rights Era institutions. We argue that to properly interpret and understand contemporary Mexican American educational attainment, it is necessary to account for the early-vintage contexts of schooling, which ranged during the Industrial

Era from ethnocentric and integrative (California) to racialized and exclusionary (Texas). Up to now, owing to limitations in available data, these historical influences have remained invisible to social scientists. We close our background chapter by introducing new data that allow us to test our ideas empirically.

Chapter 3 explores the experiences of Industrial Era immigrants of European origin, who provide an example of how integration is possible under the right circumstances, even for socially marginalized immigrants with few resources. We begin with an in-depth look at the challenging experiences of the Industrial Era immigrant generation, the sociocultural and economic contexts into which they were received, and the pessimistic and alarmist views espoused by scientists and elites at the time about these groups' impact on American society. Next, using unique longitudinal census data, we report new empirical estimates of intergenerational mobility in educational attainment by the offspring of European-origin immigrants of this era. We find especially rapid mobility over the twentieth century among the descendants of Industrial Era European immigrants, despite their parents' low levels of formal schooling. These mobility estimates are somewhat distinct from those in previous studies, in that they suggest a more accelerated pace of Industrial Era assimilation than was previously understood. As adults, the children of the Southern, Central, and Eastern (SCE) European immigrants, the second generation, nearly met or even surpassed the average level of educational attainment of their native-born, white American peers. Even the most disadvantaged of the SCE European groups—like the Italians—exceeded white native levels of schooling by the third generation (grandchildren). We conclude the chapter by summarizing the most common explanations posited by social scientists for this seeming mobility paradox, including the expansion of the American public school system prior to World War II, and the postwar expansion of higher education. These educational expansions worked in tandem with other massive government investments in Americans' human capital and prosperity to level the playing field in the pursuit of opportunity—at least for white Americans.

In chapter 4, we turn our attention to the early-vintage Mexican immigrants who were the Industrial Era peers of SCE European immigrants, but who faced much greater barriers to integration. A review of the historical literature on the experiences of early-vintage Mexican Americans reveals that they were subjected to discrimination and racial suspicion similar to that described in the many histories of Industrial Era immigrants from Southern and Eastern Europe. Mexican Americans, however, did not experience the same rapid intergenerational mobility as the SCE European groups observed in chapter 3. By adulthood, the grandchildren (third generation) of early-vintage Mexican immigrants registered an average disadvantage in educational attainment of one and a half years, a gap that is nearly twice the disadvantage experienced by their African American contemporaries. As mentioned earlier, much of the Mexican educational disadvantage stems from the Jim Crow institutional context of pre–Civil Rights Era Texas (that is, pre-1950), where Mexicans and blacks were excluded from accessing opportunities for upward mobility. In contrast, the Mexican second generation fared much better growing up in California and the upper Midwest, two migrant destinations that, unlike Texas, were heavily influenced by Progressive Era philosophies emphasizing Americanization through formal education.

In chapter 5, we give more systematic focus to the ideas gleaned from the historical accounts of Industrial Era immigration discussed in chapters 3 and 4. The disadvantages for Mexican Americans were particularly glaring in Texas, but educational outcomes were better and much more similar to those of native whites among the Mexican American families who left Texas and moved to places like Michigan, Illinois, and California. In this chapter, we explore what these places did to help equalize outcomes. The American system of public schooling is commonly perceived to be a "leveling" institution, in that it aims to provide all Americans, regardless of their social class or ethnoracial identity, with the requisite training and knowledge to pursue occupational and economic opportunities. We find strong evidence that schools leveled outcomes for the early-vintage Mexican children of immigrants. Using a newly constructed dataset that measures county-level per capita schooling expenditures from 1920 to 1946, we find that ethnoracial inequality in adult educational attainment varied substantially depending on the average level of public school investment in the places where second-generation Industrial Era children grew up. In counties with high per capita investments—which also happens to be those counties where the Progressive and Americanization movements were strong—the attainment of the early-vintage Mexican American second generation closely resembled that of their native white peers. In contrast, we see large ethnoracial gaps in attainment, and lower levels of attainment overall, in counties where school investment was relatively low.

In chapter 6, we explore whether Mexican Americans' opportunities have improved over time. We first review Mexican Americans' struggle for civil rights and the series of school reforms that followed, particularly in Texas and California. Then we compare the integration of Mexican Americans by vintage and across regions. Opportunities appear to have improved for Mexican American children across the twentieth century. Middle- and later-arriving vintages of Mexican Americans who came of age after the civil rights reforms of the 1950s and 1960s had educational mobility patterns that look much better than those of earlier Mexican American vintages and that were similar to those experienced by earlier vintages of Italians. Additionally, the large regional differences in educational attainment that were seen among early-vintage Mexican Americans started to level out among later vintages.

Chapter 7 concludes the book by summarizing the key contributions of our study and considering their broader implications for research and policy today. We highlight four lessons from the study: First, immigrants' starting points—their relative social positions upon arrival—are relatively unimportant for the eventual success of their descendants. It is important not to underestimate immigrants today. Second, structural racism has had long-lasting negative impacts that trickled down from parents to their children and grandchildren, as happened with early-vintage Mexican Americans. Third, expansions in schooling and other opportunities have helped to level the playing field across groups, including among Mexican Americans who arrived during the post–Civil Rights Era. Finally, the phenomenon of "third generation delay" is an artifact of Mexican Americans' exclusion from educational opportunity in Texas prior to the Civil Rights Era and *is not* an indicator of *present-day* downward assimilation. Throughout this discussion, we consider the ways in which America may be backsliding and whether we are at risk of repeating the mistakes of the past. Going forward, can the nation be at least as successful at integrating poor non-white immigrants as it has been in the past?

~ Chapter 2 ~

Mexican Americans as a Bellwether of Post-Industrial Integration

As we noted in the opening chapter, our focus on the integration of Mexican Americans derives from the fact that this immigrant group serves, for social scientists, policymakers, and everyday Americans, as a harbinger of the future of immigration. Their experiences and outcomes seem to provide a glimpse into how mass immigration will impact American society in the coming decades. Whether one is optimistic or pessimistic about the eventual integration of Mexican Americans is strongly tied to one's views of the nature of racial inequality in American society and the capacity of the nation as a whole to change.

Throughout this book we distinguish between immigrants of the Industrial Era and those of the contemporary era. Industrial Era immigrants are those who arrived, overwhelmingly from Europe, between about 1880 and 1920, by which point Congress effectively halted legal immigration to the United States. Immigrants of the contemporary era (sometimes referred to as "post-1965" or "post-industrial" immigration) are those arriving in the country since the landmark Immigration and Nationality Act of 1965 set in motion a new period of mass immigration that has now continued uninterrupted for about sixty years.

We also distinguish between three different institutional periods that had distinct impacts on the patterns of integration experienced by the offspring of these two periods of mass immigration. Offspring coming of age in the pre–Civil Rights Era, before 1950, faced an institutional context in which ethnic and racial discrimination in employment, housing, and opportunities for upward mobility were legal. During this period, such opportunities and the barriers to accessing them also varied considerably from state to state. The Civil Rights Era (1950–1970) saw the rise of social movements demanding equal access to opportunities for blacks, Mexican Amer-

https://doi.org/10.7758/fhka5464.8135

icans, and other minority groups. Likely due to increased federal involvement and investment, the opportunity structure became more uniform, nationwide, during this period. The post–Civil Rights Era (1970–present) witnessed the implementation and institutionalization of civil rights legislation protecting minority groups from discrimination in schooling, employment, and housing.

Before we proceed with our account of the integration of Mexican Americans and what it means for opportunity in America, we need to provide some background on how others have thought about this topic and how our approach differs. In this chapter, we introduce the basic theoretical approaches that social scientists have used to understand immigrant assimilation, and we discuss how these ideas have been applied to the case of Mexican Americans. Next, we discuss one of the key ideas advanced in this book, namely, that what we call "vintage heterogeneity" has made it difficult to get an accurate picture of Mexican Americans' integration. Finally, we describe the novel data we use; these data enable us to see this type of heterogeneity and thus identify both when and where Mexican Americans had the greatest opportunities and were therefore the most likely to become integrated into the American mainstream.

Theoretical Perspectives on Immigrant Integration

Industrial Era European Ethnic Assimilation

What happens when immigrants move into a host society? Some of the earliest systematic social science thinking about immigrant integration—or "assimilation"—was based on observations of the Industrial Era immigrants in the United States. The quintessential model of the period, as articulated by Milton Gordon in 1964 in *Assimilation in American Life*, described a steady upward or linear march in social mobility and integration with each descendant generation.[1] This linear ascension began with the adoption of American norms and customs and proceeded through a series of stages stretching across an immigrant group's multiple generations. This process of acculturation in turn opened up opportunities for structural assimilation, by which Gordon refers to the entrance of immigrants (and more likely their offspring) into the various groups and institutions comprising the nation's social structure, like clubs, schools, and workplaces. Because structural assimilation brings the descendants of immigrant groups into more frequent contact with others, it yields to a final set of more intimate forms of integration, such as intermarriage, and ends with a decline in prejudice and discrimination against them and the complete civic integration of their ethnic groups into the national society. In sum, Gordon's model describes the intergenerational process through which European immigrant groups transitioned from a socially marginalized population akin to racially excluded groups to working-class white ethnic groups that ultimately came to identify as simply white, middle-class Americans.[2]

As we will demonstrate in chapter 3, this model of linear assimilation appears suitable to explain patterns of Industrial Era assimilation for European immigrant groups. However, the linear assimilation model proposed by Gordon did not appear to characterize the mobility patterns for non-European immigrant or ethnoracial groups of the same period, notably African Americans, Indigenous/Native Americans, and Mexican Americans.[3] Writing in the early 1960s, Gordon speculated that the slower pace of mobility and assimilation experienced by non-European groups was likely due to the especially high levels of racial animus and discrimination displayed by the U.S.-born population toward these groups. Nevertheless, he appeared to assume that the model of ethnic group assimilation developed to explain the integration of Industrial Era European immigrant groups also would apply to the nation's nonwhite minorities, even if the process unfolded more slowly for them.

Social scientists' interest in immigration and assimilation waned for decades after the publication of Gordon's seminal text on assimilation. Concerns over social integration shifted to the problem of race and a series of urban crises that swept across American cities, starting in the 1960s and proceeding through the remaining decades of the twentieth century.[4] Rampant discrimination against blacks in the housing market left African Americans who had fled the Jim Crow South earlier in the century isolated in inner-city neighborhoods at precisely the same time that deindustrialization, suburbanization, and "white flight" from cities nationwide were precipitating the calamitous loss of both jobs and tax revenues.[5]

However, reforms to federal immigration law in 1965 led to dramatic increases in immigration, primarily from non-European countries. Social scientists' interest in immigrant integration was reinvigorated as the social and demographic impacts of post-1965 immigration began to be felt, first in large urban immigrant gateways and then, by the end of the millennium, throughout the nation.[6] In 1970, approximately three million children under age twelve had at least one immigrant parent or were themselves foreign-born, and well over half (58 percent) of these immigrant children came from European backgrounds.[7] By 1990 the number of immigrant children had nearly doubled, to 5.8 million, and only 27 percent of them reported European origins. Fully two-thirds of immigrant children in 1990 were Latin American (42 percent) or Asian (22 percent).

Amid this rapid demographic change, sociologists returned to the Industrial Era of immigration and Gordon's linear assimilation model for lessons that might help predict what assimilation might look like, in comparison to the Industrial Era, in a post-industrial America. In this context, might today's Latino working-class immigrants follow the same pathways as the Italian immigrants of the Industrial Era in a process of integration similar to that described by Gordon's model? Many of the theoretical revisions of Gordon's assimilation model are motivated, implicitly or explicitly, to answer this question.

Modern Perspectives on Immigrant Integration

Modern versions of integration theory are typically lumped into one of two broad schools of thought: "new assimilation" or "racialization." Although these terms crudely oversimplify the nuances of the two theoretical approaches, they are often juxtaposed as offering diverging optimistic or pessimistic views of contemporary integration dynamics and predictions about intergenerational mobility in the future. This divergence revolves primarily around each theory's assumptions about the nature of racial boundaries in post-industrial America.

The prominent optimistic view is articulated by new assimilation theory, developed by sociologists Richard Alba and Victor Nee in research articles during the 1990s as well as in their 2003 canonical book, *Remaking the American Mainstream.*[8] New assimilation theory predicts a general repeat, if in modern form, of the Industrial Era integration experience owing in large part to protections against discrimination and prejudice provided by the institutionalization of American civil rights laws (which were enacted because of the mobilization of ethnoracial groups themselves). The idea is that, in the post–Civil Rights Era context, the boundaries delineating "mainstream" America will expand over time to include the ethnically and racially distinct offspring of post-1965 immigrants. This boundary-blurring is expected to be similar to the eventual acceptance of the offspring of European immigrants as "white" in the Industrial Era. Some scholars working in this tradition have suggested that in post–Civil Rights Era America, especially in contexts and institutions that value diversity as an end in itself, the children of immigrants may enjoy a "second generation advantage."[9] In any event, perspectives within the new assimilation framework tend to expect contemporary groups like Mexicans to follow in the footsteps of poor European immigrant groups from a century before, even if acceptance into the mainstream takes a bit more generational time.[10]

In contrast to new assimilation theory, racialization theory tends to be more pessimistic. Its far different assumptions about racial boundaries in America lead to dire predictions about the integration of many post-1965 immigrant groups. Racialization perspectives emphasize that post–Industrial Era immigrants from places like Latin America, the Caribbean, and Asia are received by an American society that is rigidly stratified along ethnoracial boundaries.[11] Scholars working in this tradition caution that the parallels between the Industrial Era and post-1965 immigration contexts are not nearly as strong as assimilation perspectives might suggest.[12] They point out that the European immigrants were white "by law," meaning that they had access to the same legal and civil rights as other white citizens.[13]

Therefore, from the racialization perspective, the assimilation of the Industrial Era European immigrant groups is seen not as an example of a major shift in racial boundaries dividing whites from nonwhites. Rather, the integration of Industrial Era immigrant groups is best understood as a cultural shift, whereby the mainstream, largely Protestant culture dominant in America prior to the industrial revolution expanded to accommodate the ethnic practices and Catholic and Jewish religious traditions of groups that were already accepted as legally and socially white. The inclusion of these groups in the federal government's mobility-inducing post–World War II investment projects, and the simultaneous exclusion of nonwhite groups, institutionalized a system of racial stratification.

The American racial stratification system growing out of the Industrial Era features prominently in the leading theory of assimilation within the racialization school of thought. Working in the context of highly publicized "urban problems," such as crime, gang violence, and the crack epidemic, sociologists Alejandro Portes and Min Zhou articulated a theory of "segmented assimilation."[14] This theory predicts that contemporary integration patterns depend on variations in immigrants' contexts of reception and the ways in which these contexts "racialize" the experiences of the second generation. Integration patterns are expected to be bifurcated, reflecting the nation's racially unequal playing field, a reality that stands in stark contrast to the "only in America" immigration narrative. The children of highly skilled immigrant groups, or groups otherwise favorably received by the American government and society, are expected to rapidly join the American middle class, or the mainstream. Conversely, groups that arrive in a negative or hostile context of reception and subsequently undergo a process of racialization are likely to be integrated into American society as marginalized racial groups.[15]

As alluded to in the first chapter, the most dire prediction made by racialization theory—and the prediction that has attracted the most attention among scholars and discussion among policymakers and pundits—is the hypothesis predicting downward assimilation. This hypothesis posits that the systemic barriers facing the children of nonwhite post-industrial immigrant groups will lead to the formation of a new "rainbow underclass." The term "underclass" is often attributed to the work of sociologist William Julius Wilson, who described and explained black poverty and the social dislocations that emerged in isolated neighborhoods in deindustrializing cities beginning in the 1960s.[16] The concept was hotly debated by scholars of urban poverty, and some sociologists at the time argued that Latinos did not constitute an underclass.[17] Nevertheless, Portes and his colleagues employed the underclass model in predicting downward assimilation for certain immigrant groups such as Mexicans.

In sum, new assimilation and racialization predictions for post–Industrial Era immigrants diverge primarily over assumptions about the rigidity of the nation's racial boundaries. Mexican Americans have been positioned as the ideal case to test these competing hypotheses and thus serve as a bellwether for future patterns of integration among low-skill immigrant groups. As noted in the opening chapter of this book, however, empirical research focused on the integration and mobility of Mexican Americans paints a very mixed picture that does little to tell us which theoretical perspective is correct.

Mexican Americans' Changing Contexts of Racialization and Mobility

A problem that arises from the tendency to view Mexican American mobility patterns as a bellwether of post-industrial integration and opportunity is that Mexican immigration is not strictly a phenomenon of the post-1965 era. Most contemporary immigrant groups arrived after the 1965 Immigration and Nationality Act, and even the earliest arriving among them have produced only two adult generations to date. The starting points for these groups are situated entirely in the post–Civil Rights Era context (that is, post-1970). Conversely, many U.S.-born Mexican Americans today are members of the third or fourth generation, which trace their American roots to pre–Civil Rights Era historical contexts (that is, pre-1950).[18] Their family mobility trajectories have been shaped by distinct social, political, and economic forces that are no longer present for the immigrant groups that made their start in a post–Civil Rights Era America.

This issue of the historical diversity of immigration experiences for Mexican Americans is especially complicated when considering the meaning of race. Speculation about the nature of racial boundaries and Mexican Americans leads one immediately to the question: Which set of racial boundaries? Today's or those that emerged in the context of the Industrial Era? And if the latter, are we referring to Mexican American integration in the context of Progressive Era California or Jim Crow Era Texas?

A sociological maxim—buffeted by advances in genetic science over the last several decades—holds that races are socially constructed categories that are specific to the political and economic contexts in which they occur. Therefore, the meaning and salience of race is fluid from one context to another (two points in time or two places in the same period, for example). This fluidity is captured in the term "racialization," which implies a process through which a group of questionable status (for example, new immigrants in urban contexts, or freed slaves in the Reconstruction Era South) comes to be defined (or not) as inherently inferior and consigned to a status of deep marginalization. Racialization occurs when an inferior racial status is *institutionalized* and racial inequality comes to be seen throughout the society as natural, or at least morally justifiable. Thus, different political-economic institutional contexts will give rise to group boundaries that vary in meaning and salience.

We raise these points because they are central to the debate between contemporary integration theories, which disagree about whether Mexicans are being integrated into American society as an upwardly mobile ethnic group or as a socially excluded racial group. To fruitfully contribute to this debate, we argue here that it is essential to understand the institutional contexts in which Mexican migration began during the Industrial Era. It is especially important to ascertain whether these starting points were anchored in California or Texas, and how these two contexts compared to the urban industrial settings of the North in which the European immigrants were so heavily concentrated. We then can link these institutional starting points to Mexican American individuals' educational attainment multiple generations later and thus quantify the legacy effect that their distinctive experience of racialization has had on the patterns of disadvantage observed today.

To provide further clarity to historical contexts of racialization for Mexicans, we build on a helpful distinction, articulated by sociologist Charles Hirschman, between the ideologies of ethnocentrism and racism. He argues that ethnocentrism is a natural human aversion to difference that is likely to have been with us for a very long time. Importantly, ethnocentrism "is a product of socialization into the beliefs and practices of one's own society, seeing them as natural and, by contrast, seeing the behavior and culture of those who are different as unnatural."[19] Because ethnocentric beliefs are rooted in socialization and culture, boundaries separating "us" from "them" are permeable. Out-group members can become in-group members by accommodating their beliefs and cultural practices and socializing younger generations accordingly. Conversely, Hirschman argues, the distinctive ideology of racism emerged in human society only in the last few centuries as a way for nations to justify and naturalize European colonial projects. He defines racism as "the belief that all humankind can be divided into a finite number of races with differing characteristics and capacities because of their genes or other inherited biological features."[20] Unlike the fluid boundaries created within an ethnocentric system of beliefs, racial boundaries are drawn by nature and cannot be traversed. "They" can never join "us" because it is genetically and biologically impossible.

We build on Hirschman's schema in arguing that Industrial Era America consisted of both ethnocentric and racist institutional contexts, depending on where in the country one was born and raised. Immigrant-dense states such as Massachusetts, New York, Illinois, and California were at the forefront of the nation's expanding public school system, fueled by the Progressive and Americanization movements and animated to a considerable degree by ethnocentric views and approaches to integrating immigrant populations into the national fabric.[21] By contrast, the Jim Crow South was not only slow to modernize and fund its school system but was also socially and institutionally organized according to a racist logic, ideologically juxtaposed to the integrative goals of Americanization.

As we aim to show in this book, failing to account for these historical factors in research on Mexican American integration runs the risk of drawing biased conclusions about the nature of contemporary integration patterns and the ethnoracial boundaries that produce them. To highlight this problem further, we return to the case raised in chapter 1, that of Mexican American third-generation delay. This research finding has heavily influenced thinking about contemporary Mexican American integration.

Third-Generation Delay in Mexican American Educational Assimilation

In 2013, amid debate over a proposed bill in the U.S. Senate that would have regularized the status of eleven million undocumented residents and provided more pathways for additional legal migration, social scientists' concerns about Mexican American third-generation delay were featured prominently in the opinion pages of the *New York Times*. In "When Assimilation Stalls," Ross Douthat urges readers toward a cautious reassessment of the assumption that America remains a nation capable of integrating large flows of low-skilled immigrants.[22] He cites the same research discussed in the first chapter, showing a delay in educational progress among third- and later-generation Mexican Americans, and he connects these findings directly to concerns over the emergence of a "rainbow underclass," the dire prediction of segmented assimilation theory.[23]

As is customary among more conservative observers of immigration, Douthat attributes third-generation delay and concerns about a new immigrant underclass not to structurally embedded racism but rather to an "American economy [that] has changed in ways that make it harder for less-educated workers to assimilate and rise." In this interpretation, Douthat echoes George Borjas's influential idea that the "quality" of post-industrial immigrant cohorts (meaning their skills, abilities, and education) is declining.[24] These concerns about intergenerational delay and downward assimilation reinforce worries about an emergent underclass, such as those expressed by Samuel Huntington when he urged, "The persistent inflow of Hispanic immigrants threatens to divide the United States into two peoples, two cultures, two languages."[25] Ultimately, Douthat's argument underscores the impact that the finding of third-generation delay and concerns over downward assimilation have had on immigration-related opinion and policy proposals. It also makes clear that research on Mexican American integration carries implications that extend well beyond academic debates over contemporary assimilation.

Figure 2.1 *Third-Generation Delay in Mexican American Educational Progress, Men Ages Twenty-Five to Fifty-Nine, 1996–1999*

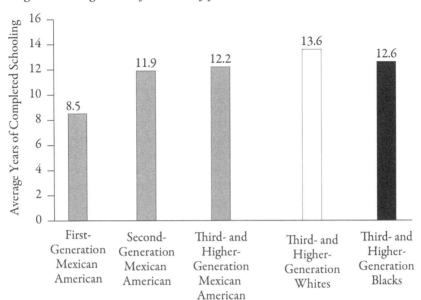

Source: Adapted from estimates presented in Grogger and Trejo 2002, table 2.3, p. 12.
Notes: The figure reports the average number of years of educational attainment among men aged 25–59. In the original table, attainment is shown for "recent" (8.6 years) and "earlier" immigrants (8.4 years). The 8.5 years presented for first-generation Mexicans in the figure represents the midpoint of the two immigrant groups.

Still, social scientists have urged caution when interpreting observed patterns of third-generation delay, especially in studies using cross-sectional data (that is, data collected at a single point in time). In the first chapter, we discussed the study demonstrating Mexican American third-generation delay by economists Grogger and Trejo, who used a cross-sectional sample from the Current Population Survey (CPS).[26] To illustrate social scientists' concerns about this approach, we reproduced, in figure 2.1, findings from one of that study's tables. The figure shows mean years of completed schooling for three generations of Mexican-origin men—the first, second, and third or higher—as compared to third- or higher-generation whites and blacks, ages twenty-five to fifty-nine. The CPS, a survey designed and administered by the U.S. Census Bureau, measures immigrant generations by probing respondents about their place of birth and their parents' places of birth. These data allow the creation of "clean" first (foreign-born) and second (immigrant parent) generations. However, because the CPS does not ask respondents about their grandparents' places of birth, it is impossible to precisely define generations beyond the second. Thus, analysts must lump all generations beyond the second into a single, *third-plus* generation, which includes the grandchildren, great-grandchildren, and so on, of Mexican immigrants.

Based on Grogger and Trejo's analysis, we see clearly notable progress between the first and second generations for Mexicans, from 8.5 years of schooling in the first immigrant generation (educated in Mexico) to 12 years in the U.S.-born second generation (figure 2.1). However, this progress stalls out in the third and later generations, which average just 12.2 years. This level of attainment fails to close the gap between Mexican American men and their native counterparts by falling about half a year short of the attainment reported among African Americans and leaving a 1.5-year gap in schooling when compared with U.S.-born whites.

One immediate limitation of the results just described is that immigrant integration is a process of intergenerational change *within immigrant-origin families*.[27] Cross-sectional designs simulate this change using what demographers refer to as "synthetic" generations, which are merely approximations of family generations (see figure 2.1). The individuals included in the first generation are not the *actual* parents of the second generation. Some cross-sectional designs attempt to more closely approximate parent and child cohorts by adjusting the ages of the generations, but that is not the case in figure 2.1, in which all of the generation groups presented are ages twenty-five to fifty-nine.

Another limitation in the approach graphed in figure 2.1 is the fact that the attainment of the first two generations was shaped by recent, post–Civil Rights Era immigration contexts. The third-plus generation, however, inherited an educational legacy from Mexican immigrant family members integrated into pre–Civil Rights Era contexts. Being unable to disaggregate the multiple generations contained within the third or higher generations, analysts cannot adequately account for those historical influences on educational attainment. Since this is a major objective of this book, we further elucidate this important point by returning to the concept of immigrant vintages introduced in chapter 1.

Vintage Heterogeneity

The United States has received substantial and nearly uninterrupted flows of Mexican immigrants since the start of the Mexican Revolution in 1910, producing "vintage heterogeneity" in the contemporary Mexican American population. Our idea in using this term is not entirely new. Other sociologists have argued that the distinctive history of Mexicans—notably the continued replenishment of the population through immigration—has produced important diversity or heterogeneity that must be accounted for to understand long-running Mexican American integration patterns.[28] Of key importance to our argument here, however, is that Mexican immigration has spanned a period of history that saw dramatic changes in the extent to which opportunities were offered to whites and denied to others. Apart from the relatively small population of original residents of the annexed territory, the century of sustained immigration from Mexico has produced at least four immigrant generations in the contemporary Mexican American population. Each of these generations descends from a specific family vintage whose immigrant starting point is anchored in a particular American historical context.

We elaborate on this important point using figure 2.2, which displays hypothetical family vintages for each of the second through fourth generations of Mexican Americans living in the United States in 2020. In this example, the youngest individuals of the three vintages were born in 1990, and therefore were age thirty in 2020, and each generation is separated in age by thirty years. An individual from the early vintage—a thirty-year-old member (born in 1990) of the fourth generation—is descended from a family vintage initiated by an immigrant great-grandparent who was born in Mexico ninety years earlier and who joined the initial waves of Mexican immigrants into the country in the 1900s after the start of the Mexican Revolution. The third-generation individuals born in 1990 belong to the middle vintage: their grandparent was born in Mexico in 1930 and arrived during the 1940s and 1950s. Finally, the second-generation individuals born in 1990 are the children of late-vintage immigrants who were born in 1960 and arrived in the 1970s and 1980s.

Figure 2.2 *Family Immigration Vintages among Hypothetical Mexican Americans Age Thirty in 2020*

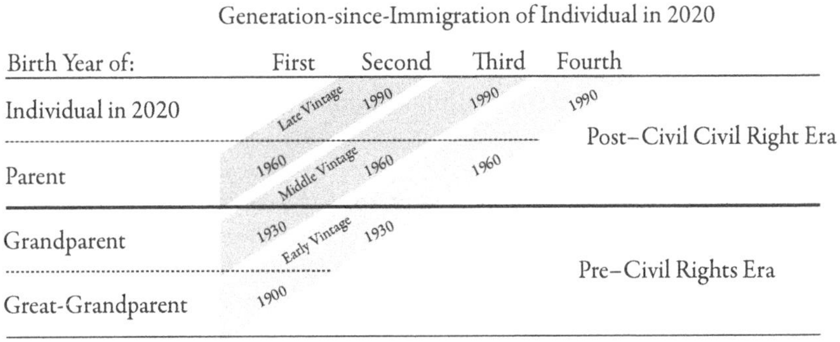

Generation-since-Immigration of Individual in 2020

Birth Year of:	First	Second	Third	Fourth
Individual in 2020	Late Vintage	1990	1990	1990
				Post–Civil Civil Right Era
Parent	1960 Middle Vintage	1960	1960	
Grandparent	1930 Early Vintage	1930		
			Pre–Civil Rights Era	
Great-Grandparent	1900			

Source: Authors' construction.
Notes: This figure depicts hypothetical scenarios assuming thirty-year birth intervals between generations.

Figure 2.3 *Estimated Year of Family Migration of Mexican American Adults by Generational Status, 2020*

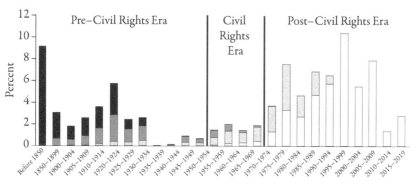

Source: Authors' estimates.
Notes: This chart shows the year of family migration of the 2020 Mexican American population by generational status. These estimates are based on the authors' demographic analysis of U.S. Census data and estimates of fertility and mortality rates for the Mexican American population (Ruggles et al. 2024).

Moving beyond hypotheticals, we show numeric estimates in figure 2.3 of the timing of migration for Mexican American adults who were age twenty-five or older in 2020. These estimates are based on our own demographic analysis of newly arrived Mexican immigrants in each decade and how their families grew and changed across generations.[29] The chart shows how each generational status is related to the timing of the family's arrival. Of Mexican Americans in the country today, nearly 10 percent are fifth- or higher generation; many of their ancestors were living in territory that was annexed by the United States in 1848. About one-quarter (24 percent) are third- or fourth-generation, and nearly all of their families immigrated to the United States before 1930. Eighteen percent are second-generation, and 75 percent of their families arrived after 1965. Finally, 48 percent are first-generation immigrants, and 99 percent of them arrived after 1965.

The fact that there is a great deal of vintage heterogeneity within the Mexican American population, as displayed in figure 2.3, is important for two related reasons. First, nearly all third- or higher-generation adults descended from immigrants who arrived before the Civil Rights Era, while most first- and second-generation Mexican Americans immigrated after that period. Because status attainment is an intergenerational process transmitted largely within families, advantages or disadvantages experienced in one generation accumulate and are passed on to shape the attainment of the next. As a result, the patterns of educational mobility or progress in early vintages are shaped to a considerable degree by historical factors and disadvantages that have little bearing on the more recent vintages that arrived after the reforms of the Civil Rights Era.

Second, earlier-arriving vintages tend to have higher rates of ethnic attrition. Ethnic attrition occurs when Mexican Americans (or any ethnic group) fail to identify their "true" national or ethnic origins in survey data. For example, people who have grandparents or great-grandparents who were born in Mexico may not always report themselves to be "Mexican American" in surveys. The tendency for ethnic identities to shift and fade across generations is strongly related to intermarriage and mixed ancestry and is very common among most groups.[30] It can cause problems, however, in research on Mexican American integration. To date, nearly all researchers interested in measuring the place of birth of each individual's grandparents or great-grandparents use survey data that rely on respondent self-reports (that is, answers to questions like, "What is your ethnicity or ancestry?"). Because of ethnic attrition, researchers end up excluding many grandchildren and great-grandchildren of Mexican immigrants from their data. Even worse, ethnic attrition is especially common among people with higher levels of education.[31] This exclusion of the most-educated people of Mexican origin thereby artificially pulls down the average estimates of educational attainment for those who continue to self-identify as Mexican American, particularly among those from earlier vintages.

In sum, the significance of vintage heterogeneity is that it might cast previous research findings showing third-generation decline in a different light. Rather than serving as an indication of where educational progress among today's Mexican American second generation is headed, third-generation decline may simply reflect historical factors that cannot be appropriately accounted for in contemporaneous cross-sectional data, and it may be exacerbated by bias stemming from selective ethnic attrition.

This study is designed around newly created, longitudinal census data that allow us to directly account for the historical opportunity structure facing Mexican immigrants and their descendants from early (pre–Civil Rights Era) vintages and to avoid ethnic attrition bias.

Data and Methodology

Linked Census Records: Immigrant Generations across the Twentieth Century (IGENS-20)

We avoid many of the problems just described because we use data that allow us to observe progress in educational attainment from one generation to the next *within families*. We use special codes created at the U.S. Census

Bureau that enable us to link individual Americans' census and census survey records over time from 1940 to the present.[32] These linkages are created using algorithms that match individual records using personal identifying information, such as name, sex, age, address, and Social Security number. Because the data we use are highly confidential, we conducted our research in a highly secure computer lab, the Penn State Census Research Data Center, and all of our results were approved for release by the Census Bureau's disclosure review board. Readers interested in learning more about the technical aspects of the linking process can consult relevant census papers.[33]

These linked datasets—which we refer to as the IGENS-20 data, for short—are ideally suited to observing patterns of intergenerational mobility. Our data begin in 1940 with children residing with their parents. The 1940 census tells us a lot about the characteristics of children's families, including where their parents were born. Because we rely solely on the place of birth of immigrants to identify the national origin of immigrants and their descendants, the data do not suffer from the ethnic attrition bias that might result if some descendants of an immigrant ethnic group no longer identify their ethnic origins in survey data. For example, the Mexican Americans in our analysis include all who descended from Mexican immigrants, regardless of their own ethnic identities. This way of identifying those of Mexican origin ensures that we include all descendants and not just those who continue to identify with the group.[34] Finally, these data enable us to compare educational attainment across more precisely measured family generations than has been possible to date. That is, we are able to distinguish between third- and fourth- or higher-generation immigrants, rather than lumping them all together into a third-or-higher generation.

We followed families over generations across four different data sources that were collected at different time periods between 1940 and the present:

1. The 1940 full-count census

2. The 1973, 1979, and 1981–1990 Current Population Surveys

3. Census 2000 (long-form data)

4. The 2001–2021 American Community Surveys

We started by identifying parents (the first family generation, or G1) who were living with at least one of their own children (the second family generation, or G2) in an earlier survey. After identifying our G1 sample, we searched for their children (G2) in a future survey after he or she had reached adulthood (age twenty-five or older). If the adult child was living with their own children (that is, the grandchildren of the G1 parents, or G3), we searched for the grandchildren in yet another future survey when they had reached adulthood. Note that the term "family generation" should not be confused with immigrant generational status. The G1 parents could be foreign- or U.S.-born. If at least one of the G1 parents was an immigrant, we classified the entire family as an "immigrant-origin" family. Otherwise, we classified the family as a "native" family.

We assembled data for three different vintages, as shown in figure 2.4. The "early vintage" consists of G1 parents who were present for the 1940 U.S. Census, whose G2 children were born between 1920 and 1940, and for whom we can link three generations. This early vintage represents Industrial Era immigrant parents who arrived between about 1900 and 1924.[35] We observe them for the first time in 1940 because it was the first census to collect information about Americans' educational attainment. The "middle vintage" consists of families for whom we were able to link only two generations and whose G2 children were born between 1960 and 1980. Most of the middle-vintage immigrants arrived between 1940 and 1980.[36] Finally, the "late vintage" consists of two-generation families whose G2 children were born between 1980 and 1994. Most of these families arrived in the United States between 1970 and 1994.

In sum, we are able to trace educational progress across generations for three immigrant vintages: (1) early-vintage immigrant families, who got their start in the country before the civil rights reforms of the 1950s and 1960s; (2) middle-vintage families, who experienced a mixture of the Civil Rights Era and the periods before and after it (although all their G2 children would have attended school after 1965); and (3) late-vintage families, whose experience in the United States occurred entirely during the post–Civil Rights Era (that is, after 1970).

The sample for most of our analyses was restricted to individuals with origins in Mexico and Italy and our two native white and black comparison groups (although we add more European-origin groups for our work in chapter 3). As shown in table 2.1, this sample includes over 4 million individuals in the early vintage, 74,000 in the middle vintage, and 559,000 in the late vintage. The large sample sizes make it possible to explore geographic variations in immigrant integration by region, and by state and county for the early vintage. Unfortunately, because the sample size declines quite a bit across family generations, we were unable to examine geographic variations for the third generation.[37]

Biennial Survey of Education, 1918–1958

The novel longitudinal census data just described allow us to observe patterns of educational mobility within families over an eighty-year period beginning in 1940. We then can estimate educational mobility separately for different historical vintages of Mexican immigrant families. Among other objectives, doing so allows us to assess whether the often reported

Figure 2.4 Data Structure of Census Longitudinal Data, by Vintage

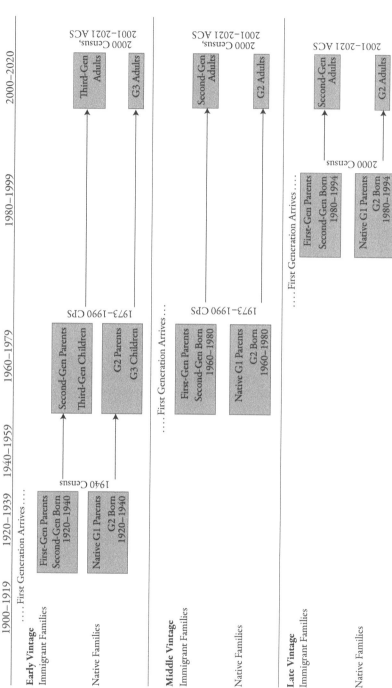

Source: IGENS-20 linked datafile, which is constructed from the 1940 U.S. Census, 1973–1990 Current Population Survey (CPS), 2000 U.S. Census, and 2001–2021 American Community Survey (ACS).

Notes: First-Gen = foreign-born; Second-Gen = U.S.-born children of foreign-born parents; Third-Gen = U.S.-born children with foreign-born grandparents; G1 = starting family generation among natives; G2 = second family generation among natives; G3 = third family generation among natives.

Table 2.1 *Sample Descriptives (Mean or Percentage) by Generation and Time Period*

	Early Vintage			Middle Vintage		Late Vintage	
	G1	G2	G3	G1	G2	G1	G2
Year of birth	1900	1929	1963	1945	1969	1956	1985
Years of education	6.8	11.8	13.9	12.3	13.8	12.0	13.5
Educational credentials							
High school	13%	69%	93%	78%	92%	75%	91%
Postsecondary	5%	29%	58%	34%	58%	36%	55%
College	2%	16%	35%	16%	32%	15%	26%
N, all groups	2,737,000	1,441,000	16,500	49,000	25,000	377,000	182,000
N, Mexican Americans	108,000	54,000	400	2,200	1,100	64,000	19,000

Source: IGENS-20 linked data.

Notes: The sample is restricted to individuals with immigrant origins in Mexico and Italy and native whites and blacks. Ethnic origin is defined based on the respondents' combined matrilineal and patrilineal lines. G1 = first family generation; G2 = second family generation; G3 = third family generation. *N*s are rounded according to disclosure rules. The Census Bureau's disclosure review board and disclosure avoidance officers have reviewed this information product for unauthorized disclosure of confidential information and approved the disclosure avoidance practices applied to this release. This research was performed at a Federal Statistical Research Data Center under FSRDC Project 2357 (CBDRB-FY22-P2357-R9408).

"decline" in educational mobility among Mexican Americans stems from pre–Civil Rights Era conditions. However, the individual census records are unable to account for the fact that at the time our study begins, on the eve of World War II, the children of immigrant families experienced local contexts of integration across the country that varied in important ways. This fact is particularly important in seeking to understand why different ethnoracial groups from the same period experienced different educational mobility trajectories. As we will show in chapter 5, children of Mexican immigrants in California and Texas faced dramatically different contexts of educational opportunity that translated into substantially lower average educational attainment in adulthood among those raised in Texas.

Our study begins in the 1940 census with children born into immigrant families in the preceding two decades. This period of American history coincides with the remarkable expansion of the nation's public education system, which we discuss in greater detail in chapter 5. The pace of public school expansion varied considerably across states prior to World War II. States with large industrial urban centers tended to have relatively well-developed systems of public education. To a much greater degree than any other major ethnoracial group in the Industrial Era, the children of Southern, Central, and Eastern (SCE) European immigrants were disproportionately concentrated in these states. Conversely, native black children disproportionately resided in the South, where states were slower to mandate and enforce compulsory schooling and develop a centralized education bureaucracy.

We account for variation in Industrial Era school contexts in our analyses using a dataset constructed by digitizing statistical tables published from 1918 to 1958 by the federal government in reports from the Biennial Survey of Education (BSE). Every other year during this period, the U.S. Department of Education (DOE) published detailed statistics, collected from school superintendents across the country, on public school enrollments, personnel, and finances for both state and city school systems. The federal government used the BSE to compile public school statistics from 1918 to 1958. Eventually, the statistics that were collected as part of the BSE were gathered under the auspices of the Common Core of Data (CCD) published annually by the DOE.[38]

The BSE data we employ in this book were extracted from publicly available reports obtained from various online archives, and they took two years to digitize and clean. This required a team of researchers and a data production process that is described in greater detail, for interested readers, in online supplement 2.4 (https://www.russellsage.org/publications/texas-style-exclusion). For our purposes, we focused on variables from the BSE that serve as reasonable indicators of material investment in the schooling of children in various states and school districts spanning the Industrial Era up to the eve of the Civil Rights Era. To our knowledge, this is among the first such efforts to digitize the BSE and integrate it into analyses of educational inequality.[39]

Group Comparisons

Beyond the wide historical scope of the data, another critical strength of the IGENS longitudinal data is that they permit direct "then-and-now" comparisons between Mexican Americans' educational attainment and that of other analytically important ethnic and racial groups. For example, the data allow us to compare, as we do in chapter 6, the intergenerational mobility patterns of Mexicans whose American experience began in the Industrial Era (then) to those of Mexican Americans descending from more recently arrived immigrants (now).

Moreover, some scholars conceptualize today's Mexican immigrants (now) as the contemporary version of working-class European immigrants of the Industrial Era, such as Italians (then). Yet, to date we are unaware of any study that directly compares Industrial Era European immigrants to Mexicans who immigrated during the same period. The IGENS data make such a comparison possible. In chapter 4, we compare Mexicans of the early vintage (then) with three other groups: native white families, native black families, and Italian American families. Native whites are an important comparison group because they represented the American mainstream during the early and mid-twentieth century. They constituted the majority group that typically occupied the highest socioeconomic and political positions and were the least likely to experience discrimination on account of race or ethnicity. Their membership in American society was never questioned. In contrast, native blacks were treated as second-class citizens with fewer legal rights. They did not have equal access to education, housing, and jobs, endured especially harsh treatment in the South, and continue to have some of the lowest educational attainments of all U.S. racial and ethnic groups today. Finally, as argued by Perlmann, Italian Americans are an important comparison group because they were similar in many ways to Mexican Americans, including their labor migration experiences and low-class origins, yet they have been successfully integrated into American society.[40] Comparing Mexican Americans with these three groups helps gauge Mexican Americans' position within the American stratification system.

Summary

What explains the rapid educational mobility experienced by the offspring of Industrial Era European immigrants? Why didn't the children of Mexican immigrants arriving in the same period experience the same rapid upward mobility? And what relevance do these facts carry for how we understand Mexican American integration today and, by extension, the future of ethnoracial inequality? As we noted in the opening chapter, these questions often have led to explanations that focus more on the individual and community characteristics of the groups themselves and less on the tremendously varying contexts across states and regions of the country in which Industrial Era immigrants were received.

In this chapter, we provided some background on how sociologists have thought about this topic and how we are contributing to this scholarship. We introduced the basic theoretical approaches that social scientists have used to understand immigrant assimilation, and we discussed how these ideas have been applied to Mexican Americans. The two major approaches, new assimilation theory and racialization theory, offer diverging optimistic or pessimistic views of contemporary integration dynamics and predictions about intergenerational mobility in the future. Much of the disagreement hinges on how the theories view the rigidity of America's racial hierarchy. Mexican immigration has served as a bellwether for understanding today's immigrant integration landscape, and the detection of "third-generation decline" in contemporary population data has fueled academic and public policy concerns about the nation's continued ability to integrate newcomers who arrive with low levels of education.

Next, we discussed a key concept for our book, which we refer to as "vintage heterogeneity." America has been receiving cohorts of Mexican immigrants almost continuously since the 1910s. Thus, the family histories of contemporary Mexican Americans are likely to have varied significantly depending on the historical era and location in which their Mexican immigrant ancestors were originally situated. As we argue, most contemporary social science research on Mexican American integration has failed to account for vintage heterogeneity, and that oversight is likely to have led to biased findings and overly pessimistic assessments of social mobility by researchers and policymakers.

Finally, in the third section of this chapter, we introduced two new sources of data that we employ in this book: linked census data extending from 1940 to 2021 and archival information about public investment in schools from 1918 to 1958. These data allow us to measure and account for vintage heterogeneity when estimating the educational mobility of the descendants of Mexican immigrants relative to other population groups.

But before documenting these patterns of mobility across vintages of the Mexican-origin population, we turn in the next chapter to observing in the IGENs data the remarkable patterns of upward mobility experienced over three generations among Industrial Era SCE European immigrant families. The rapid integration of these low-skilled immigrants serves as a high watermark for how the assimilation process can unfold under favorable conditions.

~ Chapter 3 ~

From the Tenements to the Top

The success stories often told about Industrial Era European immigrants tend to be backward-looking rather than forward-looking. Already knowing the outcome as we look back, it is easy to develop the impression that the eventual success of these immigrants was somehow inevitable, perhaps even due to built-in features of the group related to their specific cultural, religious, or social characteristics. Looking back, we tend to suffer from temporal nearsightedness. We may be unaware of the help and protections that earlier immigrants received. Our own family success stories often omit important details about the school, work, and government opportunities that were available to our great-grandparents and grandparents. Limited historical knowledge about the support received by earlier immigrants contributes to the false impression that immigrants can and should succeed on their own.

One of the aims of this chapter is to examine the circumstances of Industrial Era European immigrants from the perspective of an observer who is looking ahead and who might therefore have a sharper image of immigrants' struggles and the assistance they received. The idea is to imagine what an observer in 1940 would think if they did not know what the outcome was going to be for the millions of children and grandchildren born to Industrial Era immigrants. By no means was their success guaranteed. From the vantage point of 1940, an observer might harbor the same fears and anxieties about immigration that some people have today.

After we consider the challenges facing the Industrial Era European immigrants, we show new evidence of their success and how it unfolded across three generations. As we explain, their success was not a foregone conclusion. European immigrants did not succeed because they avoided serious challenges, or because success was somehow embedded in their culture.

https://doi.org/10.7758/fhka5464.5862

Instead, their social mobility was strongly related to a combination of beneficial circumstances, including the rapid expansion of educational, language instruction, and occupational training opportunities in the places where they settled and the fact that, as "white" or "nearly white" immigrants, they had equal access to those opportunities in those places. Our point here is to demonstrate how easy it is to underestimate the capacity of immigrants to succeed when given a fair shot.

Inauspicious Beginnings

In this chapter, we focus on the massive wave of immigration that occurred between 1880 and 1924, a group we refer to as the "Industrial Era" immigrants. During this era, one in five immigrants originated from Southern Europe (mostly southern Italy and Sicily) and 33 percent from Eastern and Central Europe (excluding Germany). In relative terms, this immigration wave was about as big as the current immigration wave today. The share of the population that was foreign-born near the end of the Industrial Era wave was about the same as in the current wave of immigration (13.4 percent in 1920, versus 13.7 percent in 2010).[1]

Industrial Era immigrants were less educated than the Northern and Western European immigrants who had arrived before them. Their reasons for leaving their homes were complex and no doubt differed from one family to the next, but like immigrants today, many emigrated in search of work and economic opportunities. In this country, they would fill industrial jobs in the manufacturing, construction, and steel industries.

For example, in the late 1800s, most people in Southern Italy and Sicily were poor tenant farmers. Some improvement in living conditions following the unification of Italy in 1871 led to rapid population growth, which in turn forced families to subdivide property into smaller and smaller plots among siblings. Small farming plots combined with lack of investment in soil conservation contributed to grinding poverty among farmers in southern Italy and Sicily. Around this same time, industrialists in northeastern urban areas of the United States were heavily recruiting manufacturing and construction workers. Many poor Italians were recruited through *padrones*, intermediaries who financed their trips and connected them to employers. Immigrants were then obligated to repay their *padrone* for steamship tickets and connections to jobs after they arrived at their destination. Like other labor migrants, such as Mexican immigrants during the middle of the twentieth century, return and circular migration was common among Italians. Men would typically emigrate first, get settled, and send remittances to their families in Italy. As many as one-third would return home, while others would send for their wives and children.[2]

Eastern European immigrants—a group that included large numbers of Ashkenazi Jews from the Pale of Settlement region of western Russia—differed from Southern European immigrants in that they tended to have higher rates of literacy and did not engage in circular migration.[3] Instead, many left their homes permanently to escape religious persecution. Nevertheless, they shared similar experiences of financial hardship. Mechanized farming practices and rapid population growth in Eastern Europe had contributed to high rates of unemployment and poverty, pushing many residents to emigrate in search of financial and social advancement. Between 1880 and the onset of restrictive immigration quotas in 1924, over two million Jews from Russia, Austria-Hungary, and Romania came to America. Many settled and worked in the urban centers of the Northeast and Midwest, such as New York, Philadelphia, Boston, Baltimore, and Chicago.

Industrial Era immigrants filled jobs in America's rapidly expanding manufacturing sector. Research studies conducted by sociologists Charles Hirschman and Elizabeth Mogford and historical economist Sukkoo Kim show that the massive influx of unskilled immigrants during the Industrial Era significantly contributed to the growth and spread of factory manufacturing in the United States, facilitating the nation's transformation from an agrarian society to a modern industrialized state.[4]

Despite their essential role in the economy and the nation's growing prosperity, Industrial Era immigrants occupied the lower rungs of America's status hierarchy. According to sociologist Richard Alba, Protestant groups from the British Isles were at the top (that is, the highest-attaining status group), other groups from Northern and Western Europe were in the middle, and at the bottom were the Southern and Eastern Europeans.[5] Many lived in crowded apartments that lacked indoor plumbing, windows, and adequate ventilation.[6] Photographer Jacob Riis documented the dangerous living conditions in the Lower East Side tenements of Manhattan in his 1890 book *How the Other Half Lives*. The exposé shocked readers, caught the attention of Theodore Roosevelt, and led to efforts to improve living conditions in these neighborhoods. Industrial Era immigrants also tended to be illiterate—for example, 36 percent of Italian immigrants could not read or write in 1910, compared with 7 percent of U.S.-born adults—and they worked in low-paying jobs in the construction, garment, and manufacturing industries.[7] In an era prior to governmental regulations and labor protections, laborers in these industries worked long hours, took few breaks, and were exposed to dangerous machinery, chemicals, dust, and fire hazards.

In response to growing political concerns about what was widely perceived as an immigration problem, Congress created a commission in 1907 to review U.S. immigration policy. Headed by Senator William Dillingham (R-VT), the commission enlisted a large team of social scientists to study all aspects of the new immigrants' social, economic, physical, and moral lives. The commission collected an unprecedented amount of data still used by historians today to understand the social and economic lives of Industrial Era immigrants. Some of the commission's members were sympathetic to immigrants' poor living conditions, and some even attributed immigrants' problems to discrimination and the unwillingness of people to welcome them into their communities.[8] Nevertheless, the report is best known for its extensive cataloging of racial groups according to their anthropomorphic characteristics and their associated character traits. The *New York Times* editorial writer Lawrence Downes quips that the Dillingham commission's report described race the way we might talk about dog breeds: "Europeans were a motley lot then. Caucasians could be Aryan, Semitic or Euskaric; Aryans could be Teutonic, Celtic, Slavonic, Iranic or something else. And that was before you got down to Ruthenians and Russians, Dalmatians and Greeks, French and Italians. Subdivisions had subdivisions. And race and physiognomy controlled intelligence and character."[9]

Despite the calls for attention to the discrimination directed toward immigrants, the commission blamed immigrants for their problems. Its overarching conclusions were that the new immigrants were incapable of being assimilated, and that a dramatic reduction in immigration was the solution to the problem. Rather than focusing on policies to help integrate immigrants, the report instead provided a rationale for immigration restrictions. The report paved the way for the passage of the 1924 Immigration Act, also known as the Johnson-Reed Act, which almost immediately cut immigration admissions to about one-fifth of their peak in 1907, eliminated most immigration from Eastern and Southern Europe, and stopped all immigration from Asia. As historian Katherine Benton-Cohen states: "The Dillingham Commission thought a lot more about how to exclude immigrants than how to incorporate them."[10]

The Tenements

Mired in poverty and a society that rejected them, Industrial Era European immigrants' prospects for success seemed limited within the historical context of the 1920s and 1930s. One place one can go to see the circumstances of Industrial Era immigrant families up close is the Tenement Museum in New York City. Founded in 1988 by historian Ruth Abram and social activist Anita Jacobson, the museum purchased an abandoned apartment building in the Lower East Side of New York, in the center of Manhattan's "Little Italy." The building had been condemned in 1935 and uninhabited ever since, so it was possible to reconstruct the details of the daily lives of those who lived there. The museum found and interviewed some of the people who resided there as children, and it conducted extensive archival research on the families, gathering information about their immigration journeys, work, family and religious lives, and children's schooling experiences. Of particular interest to us is an Italian American family, the Baldizzis, who lived in one of the tiny three-room apartments in the tenements. Their story illustrates the circumstances facing many Southern European immigrants of that era.

In the museum's account, Adolfo Baldizzi was a carpenter who immigrated from Sicily to the United States in 1923. After settling in New York, he arranged for his wife, Rosaria, to join him. Unfortunately, Rosaria was not able to immigrate legally because of the passage of the 1924 Johnson-Reed Act, which severely reduced the number of immigrants permitted from Southern and Eastern Europe. The family still managed to find a way for Rosaria to join her husband and reunite their family, but she was undocumented. Adding to the family's troubles, the Great Depression made it difficult for Adolfo to find work. Rosaria helped make ends meet by working occasionally (and without authorization) in a garment factory. The close-knit family had two children, Josefina and Johnny, who attended the local public schools. Both children noticed the ways Italians were negatively depicted in the media as criminals and gangsters. Josefina did well in school and eventually graduated from high school. She later married and had two children and several grandchildren. Unfortunately, Johnny's story did not turn out as well as his sister's. He got into fights with other children, did not perform well in school, and dropped out before completing high school. He later died at the early age of forty.

An observer in the 1930s would not have been optimistic about the chances of success for the Baldizzi family or others like them. The family faced many of the same problems that worry social scientists about today's immigrants: discrimination, persistent poverty, unemployment, undocumented immigration status, public assistance use, delinquency, and school failure. Indeed, a sociologist from today going back in time would conclude that the Industrial Era immigrants were in danger of experiencing downward assimilation into the lower class. A prominent theory in sociology, the status attainment paradigm, holds that parental status is the strongest predictor of a person's attainment in adulthood. This theory would have predicted that immigrants' low-class positions would be passed to future generations.[11] Similarly, the theory of segmented assimilation discussed in chapter 2 warns of the negative consequences of racial discrimination for the creation and solidification of American racial hierarchies. According to both of these perspectives, Southern European immigrants had little chance of upward mobility.

To elaborate, the high poverty rates among Industrial Era immigrants limited their children's access to schooling, as expected by the status attainment paradigm. In early twentieth-century America—when Adolpho, Rosaria, and other Industrial Era immigrants arrived and their children were growing up—work often started early in life and competed with schooling. Nonexistent or lax enforcement of child labor and school attendance laws allowed many children to work rather than attend school. In 1910, 56 percent of American boys and 22 percent of girls ages fourteen to seventeen reported having an occupation.[12] Despite efforts by Progressives to restrict child labor during the early twentieth century, child labor laws were resisted by employers and the courts, especially in southern states.[13]

Moreover, unskilled work offered immigrants few opportunities for promotion. Sociologist Peter Catron studied three major manufacturing firms, A. M. Byers Company, Pullman-Standard Manufacturing, and the Ford Motor Company, and found that most low-skilled immigrant workers started their work life in the same low-level position in which they ended their career decades later; they rarely were promoted.[14] Contrary to common perceptions, Catron found little evidence that these immigrants were able to work their way up within firms by climbing occupational ladders.

Even more troubling, the new immigrants were racialized.[15] This process classified and ranked them within the rapidly expanding and complex racial hierarchy in the United States, discussed earlier for its prominence in the Dillingham commission report. Different ethnic and religious groups were often described in essentialist terms that reinforced stereotypes and promoted the impression that immigrants could never change or assimilate.[16] As noted by anthropologist Nancy Foner:

> Jewish and Italian immigrants a century ago were not viewed as white in the same way that people with origins in Northern and Western Europe were: they were seen as belonging to inferior "mongrel" races that would alter the essential character of the United States and pollute the nation's Anglo-Saxon or Nordic stock. Jewish and Italian immigrants were thought to have distinct biological features, mental abilities, and innate character traits, and many Americans believed that they were physically identifiable: facial features often noted in the case of Jews, "swarthy" skin in the case of Italians.[17]

A public opinion poll conducted in 1939 asked people which nationalities made the best and worst citizens. Italians, Sicilians, and other Southern Europeans were rated the worst, Jews and Russians were rated just a little better, and Northern Europeans, such as Germans, English, Irish, and Scandinavians, were rated the best.[18]

Americans' obsession with ethnoracial rankings spilled over into the labor market and social life. It was legal to discriminate based on religion or ethnicity in the early twentieth century.[19] In fact, job ads often specified which job applicants were unsuitable, using language like "No Italians" or "No Jews or foreigners need apply."[20] It was also common for elite clubs, desirable neighborhoods, and Ivy League colleges to limit or exclude Jews.

Intellectuals were just as likely to hold these views. Social Darwinism, the theory that individuals, groups, and people are subject to laws of natural selection, gained traction among social scientists during this time and was used to justify eugenicist policies that aimed to keep Northern European groups racially "pure." It was gaining influence among fascists in Germany and Italy at that time, and the Dillingham commission report exemplified just how influential this intellectual movement had become in the United States.

According to the segmented assimilation theory, groups arriving with few resources and encountering unsupportive contexts of reception are likely to experience stagnant or slow assimilation patterns.[21] Within the early twentieth-century racial context, many Industrial Era immigrants faced discrimination and anti-immigrant backlash. Like xenophobic movements today, open hostility and resistance to the new immigrants from Southern, Central, and Eastern Europe were widespread during the first quarter of the twentieth century and are well documented in the historical record.[22] Nationalist movements such as the Ku Klux Klan gained in membership at that time by stoking fear and hatred among rural white Americans about the level of poverty, disorganization, crowding, and crime in cities where many Industrial Era immigrants settled.

Outperforming Expectations

Of course, we now know that downward assimilation did not occur. Despite their problems, the descendants of the Baldizzi family and others like them eventually integrated into the American mainstream. Those with Italian and Eastern European ancestry have been accepted into the mainstream of American society, whether we look at their socioeconomic status, their social and political inclusion as Americans, or their level of intermarriage. By the early 1980s, contemporary sociologists understood that rapid upward mobility coupled with widespread intermarriage had weakened ethnic attachments and identities to the point of rendering them symbolic[23] or optional,[24] leading sociologist Richard Alba to famously declare that the European ethnicities produced by the great industrial migration had reached their twilight sixty years after its cessation.[25]

Still, there are debates about the pace at which disadvantaged immigrant groups were able to catch up. Scholars have wondered just how long the initial disadvantages of Industrial Era immigrants lasted, and whether they ever completely disappeared. Of special concern are those from SCE Europe, who were at the bottom of the American status hierarchy. In 1970, Nathan Glazer and Daniel Moynihan argued that cultural, social, and economic differences persisted among ethnic groups and that they may not have been integrated until the third or fourth generation.[26] Likewise, in the mid-1990s, economist George Borjas claimed that immigrant group disadvantages persisted into the third generation and beyond.[27] These claims are important because they have been interpreted as evidence that there are steep and long-lasting costs of admitting low-skilled immigrants into the nation.[28] Even though Borjas's findings have been called into question,[29] his arguments continue to be used to support proposals to curtail contemporary low-skilled immigration flows.[30]

It has been difficult to assess these claims, because up until now no data have allowed researchers to definitively identify and examine the third-generation grandchildren of Industrial Era immigrants.[31] As we discussed in chapter 2, in most social science data, the third-generation grandchildren of Industrial Era immigrants cannot be clearly identified and compared with other groups. Additionally, most studies rely on the respondent's self-reported ancestry to classify the ethnic origins of third-generation immigrants. Some people do not know their family history, and even if they do, they may not have a clear ethnic origin. For example, not everyone with Italian immigrant grandparents reports themselves on census surveys as having Italian ancestry, especially if their extended family includes a mixture of ethnic groups or they are uninterested in or uninformed about their family's ethnic roots.[32]

To answer questions about the pace of assimilation, we use the IGENS-20 data—the innovative data source described in chapter 2. The findings discussed here are also reported, with minor variations, in an article we published with Kendal Lowrey.[33] We use the IGENS-20 data to follow early-vintage, European-origin families for three generations: from immigrants who arrived at the turn of the century and whose children were born between 1920 and 1940, to their adult children in the 1970s and 1980s, to their grandchildren today. Recall that the "early vintage" consists of immigrant parents of children who were born between 1920 and 1940. As we discuss in online supplement 2.1, they are representative of the Industrial Era immigrants who arrived around the turn of the twentieth century.

As we argued in chapter 1, the centrality of educational attainment in determining socioeconomic status in the United States in the twentieth century makes it the linchpin for other dimensions of immigrant assimilation.[34] Education is tightly linked to an individual's socioeconomic position as an adult,[35] their health and well-being,[36] and the life circumstances of their children.[37] For immigrants who arrived with levels of education lower than those of the U.S.-born population, the educational attainment of their children and grandchildren is a crucial marker of their structural integration into the U.S. labor force and society at large. Education provided a pathway to jobs outside of ethnic occupational niches, opportunities for learning English, wage growth, and interaction with and acceptance within the U.S. mainstream.[38]

Low Starting Points, but Rapid Integration

Most U.S. parents in 1940 had attended school around the turn of the twentieth century, before public schooling was universally available and a time when compulsory schooling laws were inconsistently enacted or enforced. By today's standards, they had very low levels of education. The native white parents in our data completed 8.7 years of schooling on average. Twenty-three percent completed high school, and about 9 percent attained some type of postsecondary education. Only 3.4 percent of native white parents in 1940 had completed a four-year college degree.

Educational attainment was even lower among early-vintage European immigrants, as shown in figure 3.1. In this chart, the squares represent the average years of schooling for first-generation European-origin immigrants, while the dotted line represents the average years of schooling of their native white contemporaries in 1940.[39]

Figure 3.1 *Educational Attainment (Years of Schooling) of Early-Vintage European-Origin and Native White Adults, by Generational Status*

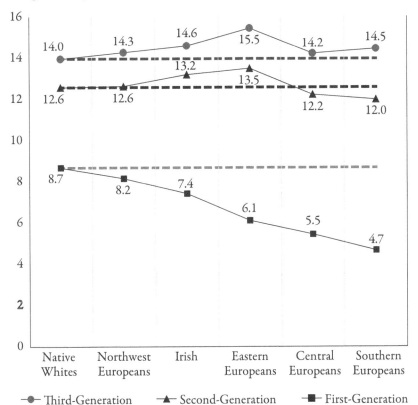

Source: Analysis based on the IGENS-20 linked data files.
Notes: The sample includes European-origin and native white adults ages twenty-five and older in the early vintage. Any views expressed are those of the authors and not those of the U.S. Census Bureau. The Census Bureau's disclosure review board and disclosure avoidance officers have reviewed this information product for unauthorized disclosure of confidential information and approved the disclosure avoidance practices applied to this release. This research was performed at a federal statistical research data center under FSRDC Project 2357 (CBDRB-FY22-P2357-R9503).

Of all the groups examined, Southern European immigrants had the lowest educational attainments in 1940. They averaged only 4.7 years of schooling, or four fewer years than native whites. The next lowest-attaining groups were Central and Eastern Europeans, who averaged 5.5 and 6.1 years of schooling, respectively. Only 5.3 percent of Central European immigrants, 3.5 percent of Southern European immigrants, and 12.4 percent of Eastern European immigrants finished high school—far less than the 22.6 percent of native whites. Finally, Northwest European and Irish immigrants had the highest levels of education among the immigrant groups, but even they fell short of native whites' levels. These educational gaps were large. To put them in perspective, today the gap in average years of schooling between native blacks and native whites is less than one year.[40]

The situation changed dramatically for the second-generation children, a group that attended school mostly in the 1930s and 1940s. This information is depicted by the triangles and dashed line in figure 3.1. The first thing to notice is that the average educational attainment increased substantially for both native white families and European immigrant families. For example, native whites in the second generation attained an average of 12.6 years of school, 3.9 more years than their parents. Additionally, 79.1 percent finished high school, about one-third attained at least some postsecondary education, and one-fifth graduated from college. This change reflects the efforts of the Progressive movement to make primary and secondary schooling mandatory, as well as the massive expansion in higher education during the postwar economic boom of the 1950s and 1960s.[41]

Just as educational attainment increased, the gaps in schooling between European immigrant and native white families narrowed considerably. Only Southern and Central Europeans continued to have significantly lower levels of education than native whites in the second generation, and even for these groups, the gap narrowed to less than a year of schooling. Additionally, the average attainment of second-generation Irish and Eastern Europeans exceeded that of native whites.

By the third generation (adults observed between 2000 and 2021), we see many reversals in the group rankings, even among those with Southern European origins. For all groups, the third-generation grandchildren of Industrial Era European-origin groups attained significantly higher levels of education than native whites. Much of their success was related to their exceptionally high rates of college completion. For example, among the grandchildren of Eastern European immigrants, two-thirds completed college (67 percent), nearly twice the rate seen among native whites (36 percent). Other formerly low-status groups also had higher rates of college completion than whites, including third-generation Central Europeans (43 percent) and Southern Europeans (44 percent). This is important because college attainment is largely a prerequisite for entry into the middle class today. Overall, those who, with respect to educational attainment, had occupied the lowest rungs of American society as immigrants in 1940 were at the highest by the second or third generation.

Accelerated Upward Mobility

The rapid integration patterns for the children and grandchildren of early-vintage European immigrants is noteworthy when we consider how low their educational attainments were when they started their lives in the United States. Parental education is the strongest predictor of children's eventual educational attainment.[42] High parental education is associated with higher income, less poverty-related stress, home environments that are more supportive of children's cognitive development, higher educational expectations and aspirations, greater parental involvement in children's schooling, and financial resources for higher education.[43] The cards are stacked against children whose parents have not gone far in school.

However, the children of Industrial Era immigrants appear to have bucked the trend. This could be seen clearly when we simulated how much more advantaged the children and grandchildren of European immigrants would have been if they had started out their lives in the United States on equal footing in 1940. To imagine this scenario, we statistically adjusted the results for parental educational attainment, other demographic factors, and place of residence.[44]

We found that if early-vintage European groups had started out in the United States with the same levels of education and lived in the same places as native whites, they would have *exceeded* native whites in schooling by the second generation. This was true for all groups. The advantages in education were 0.27 years of schooling for Southern Europeans, 0.47 years for Central Europeans, and 1.22 years for Eastern Europeans. We also found that the children of immigrants would be more likely to finish high school and to attend college than children of white natives if they had the same levels of parental education. These advantages signify that children of Industrial Era European immigrants experienced greater intergenerational upward mobility than their peers with native parents. Moreover, their advantages in educational mobility were retained in the third generation. It also means that the U.S. population may be more educated today because of the contributions of Industrial Era immigrants, their children, and their grandchildren.

Findings like these are very common and do not appear to be unique to certain European-origin groups, nor do they appear only for Industrial Era immigrants. For example, one comprehensive study conducted in 2021 by Abramitzky and his colleagues found that for dozens of Industrial Era European-origin immigrant groups, including Italians, the children of immigrants tended to experience significantly greater upward intergenerational mobility than the children of U.S.-born parents.[45] Abramitzky's study and research conducted by others on contemporary immigrants similarly finds an immigrant advantage in intergenerational mobility in education during the post–Civil Rights Era, especially for Asians and Africans, but also for some Hispanic groups, a phenomenon that sociologists of American education have labeled an "immigrant paradox."[46]

What Made Immigrants' Educational Mobility Possible?

Overall, these mobility patterns make clear that Industrial Era European immigrants experienced an accelerated form of educational mobility. In schooling, most groups caught up with native whites by the second generation and all surpassed them by the third. These findings about the assimilability of Industrial Era immigrants, particularly those from Southern Europe, should allay many of the fears people continue to have about immigrants generally.

Still, as noted earlier, this outcome would not have been predicted by sociological theories on status attainment and segmented assimilation. What made it possible? Some might look to individual-level factors, such as hard work, to understand what happened. According to this story, Industrial Era immigrants, such as Italians and Eastern European Jews, were able to get ahead through grit and perseverance, despite the challenges they faced. No doubt, there is some truth behind this story, but such a possibility merely pushes the question back a few steps. Even if it were demonstrably true that immigrants tended to have high expectations and that they tended to work harder than others to fulfill those expectations, *why* was that the case?

To answer this deeper question, we need to look at structural factors—that is, the features of immigrant groups and the social and economic contexts in which they were living. In this section, we discuss the more prominent ideas that have been advanced for understanding immigrant advantage. We first consider factors that worked to advance opportunities for all and may also have leveled the playing field for the children and grandchildren of some immigrant groups. Then we turn to arguments that seek to explain the unique immigrant advantages in these families.

A Level Playing Field

First, massive social and economic changes were occurring in the United States during the early and mid-twentieth century that increased educational attainment for all groups. As argued by Richard Alba, the rapid expansion in public schooling, higher education, and the labor market after World War II provided the structural changes that enabled a "non-zero-sum" pattern of assimilation.[47] In other words, European-origin immigrant groups were able to advance without having to outcompete or displace others located above them in the status hierarchy. For example, as part of the

New Deal and Fair Deal programs enacted to improve economic conditions, the Servicemen's Readjustment Act of 1944 (the GI Bill) was introduced to create enhanced opportunities for college attendance.[48] By 1956, 7.8 million veterans had used the GI Bill's education benefits—2.2 million to attend colleges or universities and an additional 5.6 million to enroll in other training programs.

European immigrants were very well positioned to take advantage of the educational reforms and expansions occurring in the United States in the first half of the twentieth century. They were highly concentrated in urban areas in the Northeast and the Midwest, and these were the same locations where educational reforms first took root in the early twentieth century, well ahead of other places in the country.[49] As we will discuss at length in chapter 5, public schools received greater support and were more established during the early twentieth century in these places than in other parts of the country.[50] Prior research has shown that laws making school attendance compulsory and regulating child labor, as well as public spending on education, spurred the massive expansion in education during the early to mid-twentieth century.[51]

The expansion in public schooling grew out of and was amplified by the Americanization movement, which directed its efforts specifically toward immigrants. During the first few decades of the twentieth century, state and local governments in the Northeast and Midwest, as well as some large private philanthropies and companies (such as the American Seating Company, where Jenny's grandfather worked), sought to transform the new European immigrants from "foreigners" into "Americans." It is important to recognize that this social, political, and religious movement had overtly ethnocentric goals. Sociologist Michael Olneck argues that the major motivation for the Americanizers was to replace ethnic identities with an American identity.[52] The Americanizers displayed ethnocentric bias in that they felt that their white Protestant culture and language were superior and should be adopted by the new immigrants. They provided instruction in civics and American "values," promoted individualism, and imposed English-only laws. Yet they also engaged in efforts to Americanize the children of immigrants through the expansion of public day schools, while simultaneously implementing night school programs designed to promote immigrant adults' civic integration and offer them basic education and vocational training. By imposing compulsory schooling and child labor laws and integrating children of all backgrounds in the same classrooms, the Americanizers hoped that schooling would instill a common American identity and reduce the use of non-English languages.[53]

Ironically, the ethnocentric aspects of the Americanization movement appear to have been unsuccessful. In many arenas—cuisine, the arts, and religion—Industrial Era European immigrants transformed U.S. culture rather than conform to Anglo-Saxon Protestant ways.[54] Additionally, all groups learned to speak English within a generation or two, but likely not because of the English-only laws promoted by the Americanizers. Research by economists Adrianna Lleras-Muney and Allison Shertzer shows that English-only laws were not significantly related to the rate at which immigrants naturalized or to their labor market success in adulthood.[55] Immigrants naturalized and succeeded in the labor market regardless of whether they were forced to use English.

However, the children of immigrants did benefit from the Americanization programs' promotion of school attendance. Lleras-Muney and Shertzer's research also shows that keeping children in school longer by increasing the age requirement for a child to work had a positive impact on immigrants' educational attainment and earnings in adulthood.[56] Moreover, these investments in public education at the primary and secondary levels made it possible for the children of Industrial Era European immigrants to take advantage of other opportunities throughout their lives. For example, they were primed to take advantage of the GI Bill because so many of them had graduated from high school and therefore were eligible for college. Investments in schools also made it possible for them to compete for professional positions in the rapidly expanding postwar economy.

Aside from public investments in schools, two major events may have leveled the playing field for European immigrants and strengthened the shared identities people had as Americans. The first event was the immigration hiatus that occurred during the late 1920s and 1930s. Immigration from Eastern and Southern Europe dropped dramatically after the passage of the 1924 Johnson-Reed Act, and all immigration slowed to a trickle during the Great Depression of the 1930s. This pause in immigration changed how immigrants were perceived by others. As time passed, Industrial Era immigrants eventually were replaced by their second-generation children, and then by their third-generation grandchildren. Importantly, ordinary Americans typically do not distinguish people by their generational status but instead base their stereotypes on the entire group. Therefore, as each new generation became more integrated into the American mainstream, the entire group was perceived as less foreign and more American. For Italians and other Industrial Era immigrants, the cessation of immigration for several decades probably contributed to their acceptance as Americans.

The second major event was World War II. The war effort required sustained sacrifice and massive restructuring of the nation's economy. Air raids, rations, the draft, and military service (which, though segregated racially, integrated white European ethnicities) unified the nation against a common enemy. An estimated 750,000 to 1.5 million Italian Americans enlisted to fight in the war. In one poll of Americans conducted by *Fortune* magazine in the lead-up to the war in 1938, respondents reported the most negative feelings toward the nation's geopolitical foes. About one-third of respondents reported that they felt the least friendly toward Germans, and 20 percent said that they felt the least friendly toward Japanese. Only 7 percent reported feeling unfriendly toward Italians.[57] Thus, even though many Americans of the late 1930s did not think Italian Americans made good citizens, as reported earlier in the chapter, even more harbored negative feelings about their common enemies, the Germans and Japanese. This is consistent with the argument made in the PBS documentary *The Italian Americans* that the war was pivotal in reducing the social divisions between Industrial Era immigrant groups and other Americans.[58]

Immigrant Advantages

The factors just discussed—educational expansion, the immigration hiatus, and World War II—provided common experiences that reduced social distances between groups. However, they do not explain why Industrial Era European immigrants were even more successful than their native white counterparts. For example, investment in public schools clearly raised Americans' educational attainment, but our supplemental analyses suggest that public school investment does not explain European immigrants' *exceptional* success in school above and beyond the attainment of native whites. As shown in online supplement 3.3, immigrants' children and grandchildren outperformed the children and grandchildren of native whites practically everywhere they settled, regardless of the level of educational investment in the region. To understand immigrants' unique advantages, we must examine the immigrant experience more closely.

One possibility is that the astounding increase in educational attainment between the first and second generations may not have been so astounding after all. Immigrant parents' educational attainment may have been low simply because they had fewer schooling opportunities in their countries of origin than they would have received in the United States. Simply moving to a more resource-rich environment with better schools may have contributed to greater intergenerational upward mobility for immigrant families when compared with native families. Additionally, as argued by Cynthia Feliciano and Yader Lanuza, even if immigrant parents had lower levels of education than U.S.-born parents, they may still have had more education than those in their sending communities, and their *relative* advantage within their sending community may matter more than their *absolute* level of education.[59] Having originated from a higher class, immigrant parents may have supported and pushed their children to succeed in school as much as highly educated U.S.-born parents did. We suspect that this explanation may at least partially underlie the rapid upward mobility of the children and grandchildren of Eastern European immigrants, a group composed mostly of Jewish immigrants with unusually high literacy rates (even if they had little formal schooling) compared with other Europeans.

However, it is unlikely that Feliciano and Lanuza's explanation applies to Southern European immigrants. As noted earlier, these immigrants originated from the lower rungs of society in southern Italy and Sicily in the late 1800s and early 1900s, which was itself among the poorest regions of Europe at the time. Poverty did not prevent working-age men from emigrating but most likely propelled them to do so.[60] This suggests that Italian immigrants did not come from the upper classes in their sending communities. We provide further support for this argument in online supplement 3.4.

Another, perhaps more plausible, explanation for the rapid upward mobility among Italians and other Industrial Era immigrants is that they were able to draw upon coethnic and familial experiences and resources to assist in their settlement and integration. The European groups settled in enclaves where new immigrants could live, work, and seek support from earlier-arriving coethnics.[61] Michael White and Erica Mullen's research on upward mobility among Industrial Era immigrants suggests that later-arriving groups were given a hand by earlier-arriving coethnics, enabling them to catch up more quickly than similarly low-educated U.S.-born counterparts.[62] The rise in Catholic educational enrollment, may have been one way in which this occurred.[63] To improve their education, the Catholic working class formed their own schools, which paralleled the rigor of the public schools' nonreligious curriculum,[64] yet allowed them to be culturally accommodating.[65] By adapting a model of mass schooling from the public sphere, Catholic schools were able to educate some of the least-educated populations in U.S. society.[66]

Another possible reason for immigrants' accelerated upward mobility is that they and their children were making a fresh start when they moved to the United States. Forced to make new choices about nearly all aspects of life, they may have been more likely than natives to take advantage of the opportunities in their new homes and communities. For example, without strong ties to specific neighborhoods and cities, they relied on social networks to learn about and move to places that offered the greatest opportunities.[67] Likewise, their children may have felt the freedom to pursue career paths that were not available to their parents and grandparents. In contrast, inertia kicks in for people who are less inclined to move for opportunities, and they may find themselves accepting less lucrative jobs to remain close to home. Additionally, many immigrant groups lacked occupational mobility ladders and faced discrimination within the mainstream business world.[68] Ironically, this may have pressured children of immigrants to forge new paths, take risks, and innovate. For example, Charles Hirschman documents the dominance of immigrants and children of immigrants in the film and music industries throughout the twentieth century in the United

States.[69] He argues that this resulted from their need to take risks. Like the arts, higher education may also have offered an important new pathway to success that was available to the children of immigrants.

Still another explanation is that the children of immigrants often feel obligated to fulfill their parents' dreams for upward mobility in return for the sacrifices they made in moving to the United States. This is sometimes referred to in integration studies as the "immigrant bargain."[70] Immigrant families often view upward mobility as a family project. Parents make sacrifices to move to the United States so that their children will have greater opportunities than they would have had in their countries of origin. In exchange for their parents' sacrifices, their children may feel pressure to work long hours to contribute to household income or support the family business. They may also fulfill their obligations by pursuing secondary and post-secondary educational credentials, particularly where higher education is available, affordable, and recognized as having clear financial benefits. As noted earlier, such circumstances started to emerge, especially for men, during the economic and educational expansion in the decades following World War II. Children of immigrants may have felt more pressure than children of native parents to take advantage of these expanding educational opportunities.

Indeed, pressure to succeed continues to be observed among present-day immigrant families. For example, Grace Kao and Marta Tienda suggest that some of the characteristics common to immigrants, such as optimism about searching for new opportunities via migration, are responsible for their increased success.[71] Jennifer Lee and Min Zhou have found that Chinese immigrant families promote educational success through family values that place high emphasis on educational performance and impose extremely ambitious and narrowly defined standards for what is considered "successful"—for example, an Ivy League education followed by a career as a doctor or lawyer.[72] Lee and Zhou also argue that this phenomenon is unique to immigrants and not tied to the culture of immigrants' countries of origin. For example, they show that the outstanding performance of the children of Chinese immigrants is not evident among Chinese living in China. Although little systematic knowledge is documented about the level of pressure to succeed felt by the children of Industrial Era European immigrants, there are plenty of anecdotal examples in literature, film, and other historical materials about how Italian and Jewish families pressured their children to succeed for the honor and reputation of the family.

Summary

Early-vintage European immigrants succeeded beyond expectations. When they arrived in the United States from Southern, Central, and Eastern Europe around the turn of the twentieth century, they started out near the lowest socioeconomic position of society. Like the Baldizzi family, they had much lower levels of education than native whites and earlier-arriving immigrants from Northwest Europe, faced discrimination in labor and housing markets, and were treated socially in many ways like inferior racial groups. Many observers at the time, such as the authors of the Dillingham commission report, blamed immigrants' hardships on the groups themselves, believing that they were unassimilable. These observers did not think that the new immigrants would fit in, and they could not imagine that the American mainstream would expand enough to include them. These fears led the United States to pass the 1924 Johnson-Reed Act, which severely restricted admissions of the "new" immigrants from Southern and Eastern Europe. Still, despite their limited resources and poor treatment, Industrial Era immigrants quickly assimilated into the American mainstream. By the second generation, most European-origin groups had attained educational levels that were on par with those of white natives, and by the third generation all had surpassed them.

In hindsight, it might be tempting to attribute this success to the inherent qualities of the Industrial Era European groups themselves as naturally hardworking risk-takers who set very high expectations for themselves and their children. The problem with these characterizations, however, is that they are stereotypes easily manipulated to confirm preexisting beliefs. For example, during the early twentieth century, when Americans were worried about immigration changing American society for the worse, Southern Europeans were stereotyped as criminals who were suited only for manual labor. Now that they have become successful, however, they are stereotyped as hard workers with strong family values. Either way, these essentialist explanations for the success (or expected failure) of Industrial Era immigrants make little sense given that we see the same pattern of rapid integration across many groups: Catholics, Jews, and Protestants; groups that experienced discrimination and those that did not; and those with both high and low class origins. Another problem is that these kinds of explanations merely beget more questions. Even if certain groups tend to behave in certain ways, we are left wondering what creates those differences. Essentialist explanations are problematic because they overlook the influence of structural factors in shaping group disparities.[73]

Indeed, there is a good chance that the success of Industrial Era European immigrants was due to a combination of structural conditions. First, these immigrants had access to public schooling during a period of educational expansion. This access leveled the playing field, making it possible for children whose parents had exceptionally low levels of education, among white children at least, to get high school degrees and to take advantage of other opportunities later in life. As Richard Alba argues, the economic expansion and progressive reforms in the years following World War II allowed immigrants to rise without displacing others above them in the status hierarchy (that is, they could experience "non-zero-sum" mobility).[74]

Second, it is crucial that Industrial Era European immigrants and their children had access to these opportunities. The major goal of the Progressive movement in the Northeast, Midwest, and on the West Coast was to educate and "Americanize" the children of immigrants. Although the Americanization movement failed to acknowledge the many benefits of cultural diversity, it ensured that all children had access to schooling regardless of ethnicity or their parents' educational level. As we discuss later in the book, the fact that the Progressive movement sought to integrate Industrial Era European immigrants rather than permanently confine them to the working class and underclass reflects the nature of the American racial hierarchy and its boundaries at the time. European ethnics, while not fully accepted as Americans on account of their religion, food, and language, were still seen as belonging to the "white" category in the eyes of the law (even if they had lower status than Northwestern Europeans) and clearly were not classified as "black."[75]

Third, immigrant families tended to have a common set of experiences that contributed to their accelerated upward mobility and outpacing of the children and grandchildren of native whites, including positive selection (especially for Northwest and Eastern Europeans), strong ethnic communities, and pressure on the children of immigrants to contribute to the family project of upward mobility (that is, the "immigrant bargain"). Given the limitations of historical social science data, it is difficult to know for certain whether these various explanations would hold up under further scrutiny. For example, because we are unable to measure the interpersonal dynamics of the immigrant families in our data, the precise connection between the "immigrant bargain" and educational outcomes remains vague. Still, the circumstantial evidence for all of these explanations is abundant. Immigrants and their children were more likely than non-immigrants to start up new businesses and to succeed in the cutthroat entertainment and arts industries.[76] Historical accounts also provide evidence about the immigrants' close-knit ethnic communities and the pressure they placed on their children to succeed.

What are the implications of these points for understanding the prospects for Mexican immigrants and their children and grandchildren? First, the story of the Italian Americans gives us a reason to be optimistic for Mexican Americans. When looking at history, we can see the many parallels between the two groups. Just as Italians eventually proved the authors of the Dillingham report wrong, it is possible that contemporary pessimists are equally wrong about Mexican Americans, particularly if the opportunities made available to Italians are also provided to Mexican Americans.

Unfortunately, as we discuss in the next chapter, during the first half of the twentieth century, Mexican Americans were racialized much more systematically than Industrial Era immigrants from Southern and Eastern Europe, especially in Texas, where a castelike racial hierarchy was rigidly enforced. The racism that Mexican Americans encountered in that state largely excluded them from schools, the key institution that typically leads to lifelong opportunities in labor markets, housing markets, and interpersonal relationships within the American mainstream. We examine these issues in detail in the next chapter.

~ Chapter 4 ~

Texas-Style Exclusion

The integration of early-vintage Mexican immigrants differed dramatically from the integration of their European-origin counterparts. In the previous chapter, we discussed the unexpectedly accelerated intergenerational mobility experienced by early-vintage European immigrants, including Southern Europeans who arrived with the lowest levels of human capital and were discriminated against in the labor market. Embedded in an ethnocentric, yet integrative context, they not only caught up with native whites but exceeded them in educational attainment by the third generation.

Early-vintage Mexican Americans had a very different experience. Although Italians and other Southern, Central, and Eastern (SCE) European immigrants were discriminated against in the labor market and endured negative stereotypes and ethnic slurs, they were not subjected to the same kind of racism as Mexicans. In a racist institutional context, the rights of Mexicans were limited more extensively than was the case for SCE Europeans, and the social distances between Mexicans and whites were far greater than those separating SCE Europeans from whites.[1]

We begin this chapter with a brief history of early twentieth-century Mexican immigration and a discussion of the relative positioning of Mexican Americans within U.S. society as ethnoracial minorities during the Industrial Era. Next, we use the IGENS-20, linked census data described in chapter 2 to compare the educational starting points and intergenerational mobility of early-vintage Mexican-origin families with those of early-vintage Italian immigrant families. We also compared the starting points and mobility patterns of Mexicans and Italians with those of their native white and native black contemporaries.

By focusing on these early-vintage groups, we shine a light on the privileges afforded to Italians and the comparative disadvantages of Mexicans

https://doi.org/10.7758/fhka5464.3939

during the Industrial Era. This comparison is not merely of historical interest. As discussed in chapter 2, Industrial Era immigrants were the grandparents of today's third and fourth generations. The older generation's experiences and opportunities are deeply connected to how well early-vintage Mexican Americans are doing today, given how group-level disadvantages and advantages are passed down in families. Therefore, understanding the disadvantages of earlier-vintage Mexican immigrants helps us explain inequality among later-generation Mexican Americans today as we examine how particular historical institutional contexts give rise to the specific intergenerational patterns presented in this chapter.

Our findings tell a clear story of marginalization for most early-vintage Mexican American families. Mexican and Italian immigrants entered the United States with similar levels of education and similar rural peasant backgrounds, yet the children and grandchildren of Mexican immigrants did not fare as well as those of Italian immigrants. Their outcomes were more like those of native blacks than outcomes for native whites, especially among those who lived in Texas. Early-vintage Mexicans came nowhere close to the accelerated mobility patterns experienced by Italians.

Early Twentieth-Century Mexican Migration

Migration between Mexico and the Southwest of what is today the United States has been occurring continuously for several hundred years. Some Mexican Americans were never immigrants but instead were living in territory that was taken from Mexico in 1848 under the Treaty of Guadalupe Hidalgo. Following the war between the United States and Mexico over Texas, the current states of California, Arizona, New Mexico, Texas, and Utah and parts of Wyoming, Colorado, Nevada, Oklahoma, and Kansas were annexed by the United States. Mexican citizens living in the annexed territory had the option to relocate on the Mexican side of the newly established border, or they could remain in place and be given American citizenship with full civil rights. Over 90 percent of roughly 80,000 Mexican nationals chose to remain, yet the descendants of this group make up a small share of Mexican Americans today. As noted earlier in figure 2.3, we estimate that about 9.5 percent of the contemporary Mexican American population descends from residents of the territory prior to annexation.

Most Mexican Americans living in the country today (90.5 percent) descend from immigrants who arrived in the United States after 1850, with the vast majority (about 88 percent) arriving during the twentieth century. Mexican immigrants trickled into the American Southwest from Mexico throughout the second half of the nineteenth century; only 13,300 Mexicans were officially admitted between 1851 and 1900, an average of 2,700 per decade.[2] Only 105,000 Mexican-born individuals were counted in the 1900 U.S. census.[3] The number of Mexican immigrants increased dramatically, however, after the turn of the twentieth century. Fifty thousand Mexican immigrants were legally admitted in the first decade between 1901 and 1910, 219,000 in the second decade, and 460,000 in the third. These figures are likely to underestimate the true number of incoming migrants because they do not include those who entered without inspection by immigration officials. Historian George Sanchez describes accounts of Mexican workers being waved through ports of entry without scrutiny from immigration officers.[4] We also can see evidence of this practice in the census figures, especially early in the century. In the first decade of the twentieth century, the growth of the Mexican-born population recorded in the census was four times the number of admissions of Mexican immigrants.

Myriad factors account for the rise in Mexican migration in the early decades of the twentieth century. Although wages were much higher in the United States than in Mexico, this differential is only part of the explanation. Advances in water irrigation that transformed large areas in southeast Texas and California's Imperial Valley into "Winter Gardens," as well as the growing agricultural and manufacturing sectors in the Midwest (for example, Kansas, Illinois, and Michigan), increased demands for low-wage labor during the early twentieth century.[5] These labor demands were at first met by immigrants from SCE Europe in the Northeast and Midwest and from China and Japan in the West. However, a series of exclusionary immigration laws—the 1882 Chinese Exclusion Act, the 1907 Gentlemen's Agreement with Japan, the Emergency Quota Act of 1921, and the even more restrictive 1924 Johnson-Reed Act—and the turmoil of World War I severely reduced these sources of labor.

Mexicans were exempted (whether by law or simply in practice) from the new restrictive immigration laws in order to appease employers who depended on a steady supply of low-wage labor. When Congress gave preference to admitting immigrants from Northern and Western Europe by enacting country-specific immigration quotas in 1921, passing even more restrictive quotas in 1924, and barring admission for anyone unqualified by race for citizenship (thus excluding Asians), it exempted the Western Hemisphere, including Mexicans. Additionally, as Sanchez notes, immigration officers along the U.S.-Mexico border tended to ignore public charge and literacy requirements when determining admissibility for Mexicans. One inspector in El Paso reported:

> We can exclude practically all of the Mexican aliens of the laboring class who apply for admission at this port as persons likely to become a public charge, for the reason that they are without funds, relatives or friends in the United States, and have no fixed destination; at the same time we know that any able-bodied man who may be admitted can immediately secure transportation to the point on the railroad where employment will be furnished him.[6]

Border patrol agents were much more concerned about keeping out poor and illiterate Chinese laborers who were trying to enter the country at its southern border.

Additionally, starting in the first decade of the twentieth century, Mexicans were actively recruited to work in the United States. At first, workers were recruited within the interior of Mexico. Sanchez describes in detail how newly constructed railroad lines that connected communities both within Mexico and from Mexico to the United States enabled labor recruiters to travel to the Mexican interior, stop at train stations in towns and villages, and recruit workers from the local area. Eventually, as word of the higher wages in the North spread throughout social networks in Mexican communities, labor recruitment in Mexico was no longer required. Historian David Montejano documents, for example, the elevation by Anglo growers and ranchers in Texas of certain Mexicans to act as intermediaries and use their social connections to recruit and manage their transient workers from Mexico.[7] As cross-border connections were made between sending and receiving communities, the practice of labor migration became self-perpetuating.[8]

Laborers were also recruited in the United States in coordination with immigration officials. According to Sanchez, some labor recruiters would stand directly outside the office of the Immigration Service.

> The agents representing the railroads and the ranches would make speeches about the delightful quarters, good pay and fine food they would have if they went to work for their company. When the promising was over, the agents would shout, 'This way for the Santa Fe,' 'This way for the Southern Pacific,' and so on, the men following the agent they thought offered the best or most benefits.[9]

As noted by Sanchez, although many of these arrangements bent or even broke U.S. immigration law, "both American officials and entering aliens understood that it was the labor needs of the American Southwest that defined Mexican migration to the United States and not laws drawn up in Washington."[10]

Finally, Mexican labor migration was often circular. Many immigrants (mostly men) would travel north to work for a season or two before returning to their homes in Mexico. This was like the experience of Italian labor migrants, among whom it was common practice to send remittances home to Italy and eventually to return there. Characteristic of labor migrants, Mexican migrant laborers often made repeated trips without their families, and some did so every year. They would bring their families with them to the United States only after they decided to stay permanently. It is difficult to know for certain how many Mexican migrants stayed in the United States, but a simple comparison of the number of admissions recorded by the Immigration and Naturalization Service (INS) and census numbers suggests that roughly half stayed. For example, during the 1920s (when the INS did a better job of recording immigrant entries), about half a million Mexicans were legally admitted to the country, but only half this number indicated in the 1930 census that they arrived during the 1920s. Our estimate that roughly half of Mexican immigrants settled in the United States is consistent with other indicators as well. In 1930, 56 percent of Mexican-born adults ages eighteen or older reported having at least one of their own children living with them (with over half of these children being under the age of five)—a good signal of an intention to stay.

When they first started arriving in the United States, many Mexican immigrants did not think of it as a permanent move. This arrangement was to the liking of U.S. employers for both economic and social reasons. They sought a source of low-wage labor they could employ in large numbers when needed and dispense with when no longer needed. Additionally, they wanted the benefits of having access to low-wage labor without the accompanying social problems of a large, impoverished population to house, clothe, and educate.

The dispensability of the Mexican labor force is clearly illustrated by their treatment during the Great Depression of the 1930s, when Mexicans encountered heightened discrimination in the tightened labor market and at the welfare office. They were cast as outsiders, unworthy of the scant jobs and resources that ought to be reserved for "Americans." Sanchez documents the story of a Chicano ex-officer in the U.S. Army who was denied jobs on account of his race:

> The supervisors come out [by the construction sites] and tell the people that are waiting to get a job to line up on one side, all the white people, and on the other side the ones that are not. Because I am of dark complexion I stay with the people of my race and of course, do not get hired because the supervisor has the order to hire only the "white people" and this is what he does.[11]

Joseph Dunn, then a state senator from California, researched this period of history when he authored and advocated for California's Apology Act of 2006. He found that President Herbert Hoover had been looking for a scapegoat for America's economic struggles when, in 1929, he announced a national program of "American jobs for real Americans." Dunn explains that this was code for "getting rid of Mexicans." Hoover's secretary of labor, William Doak, helped implement the program by working with local governments to pass laws forbidding government employment of anyone of Mexican descent (such a law was passed in California in 1931).[12] Major companies joined the effort by laying off thousands of Mexican workers.

To further this goal of returning jobs to "real Americans," local communities, with the support of Mexican consulates, "repatriated" hundreds of thousands of Mexican Americans to Mexico. We use quotes around the term because some of the deportees were U.S.-born; technically they could not be repatriated, because they had never been to Mexico before. The U.S. government did not formally deport large numbers of Mexicans. Rather, local officials and vigilante groups would pressure and sometimes even arrest Mexicans without due process and force them onto buses or trains to Mexico, regardless of their immigration status or place of birth. Ironically, the repatriation campaigns may not have achieved their goals of improving the Depression-era employment situation of U.S. natives. One study led by economist Jongkwan Lee estimated that the reduction in the Mexican population during the 1930s did not achieve the desired effect of reducing unemployment among U.S. natives.[13] Because the jobs vacated by Mexican workers were not the types sought by U.S. natives, repatriation may have even increased unemployment slightly.[14]

Ethnocentrism, Racism, and Mexican Americans' Place in American Society

American society in the early twentieth century was highly regulated by race and intensely focused on whether a person was classified as black or white. This black-white binary was challenged when large numbers of immigrants from Europe, Asia, and Latin America arrived during the Industrial Era. In the eyes of the law, were the newcomers to be treated as white? Borrowing from the field of taxonomy, which sought to classify plants and animals into species and subspecies, social Darwinists tried to describe the innate characteristics, predispositions, and abilities of diverse groups of people. Although they subdivided Europeans into different "races," they also put European immigrants into the broader "white" category, a classification that gave them the same privileges as white natives, such as the right to naturalize, live in white neighborhoods, and attend white schools.[15] In contrast, groups such as Chinese and Japanese immigrants were not classified as white and therefore were denied many basic rights, including the right to become a citizen through naturalization.[16]

Where did Mexicans fit into this racial order? To answer this question, we take a detour into the meaning and significance of race as understood by sociologists. As discussed in chapter 2, the term "race" refers to arbitrary physical differences (for example, skin tone) that groups and cultures consider significant. The salience of race for organizing and sorting individuals within a society depends on the strength of the "boundaries" that separate groups from one another. "Bright" boundaries demarcate widely recognized groups that are difficult to leave or join through intermarriage, assimilation, or social mobility, whereas "blurry" boundaries are easier to cross.[17] With the bright racial boundaries separating blacks from whites during the 1920s and 1930s, no black person, no matter how rich, educated, or talented they were, could marry a white person, attend white schools, or live in white neighborhoods.

In addition to being rigid, bright boundaries tend to be embedded in the legal system. For example, the boundaries separating whites from blacks were reinforced by the Jim Crow legal system in the South that mandated the separation of blacks from whites in all aspects of life and failed to prosecute or convict those who engaged in racial intimidation and violence. Bright boundaries separating white and black Americans also were institutionalized outside of the South in the years following World War II. For example, the establishment of a system of "redlining" in northern cities made it impossible for blacks to secure loans for homes in white neighborhoods.[18]

Finally, bright boundaries funnel societal resources and power to privileged groups. With bright boundaries between blacks and whites, schools attended by black students received less public funding than schools attended by white students; public infrastructure, such as paved roads and water sanitation, was not provided in places where black people lived; and voting rights for blacks were suppressed. African Americans were thus disproportionately excluded from realizing the full benefits of large-scale federal investments in Americans' human capital and material well-being through programs such as Social Security and the GI Bill.

As these examples demonstrate, the racial boundary between blacks and whites has been unequivocally bright throughout the twentieth century. The boundaries dividing blacks from whites were widely recognized throughout the United States, not just in the South; institutionalized by segregation and by anti-miscegenation and voter suppression laws, these boundaries determined an individual's access to schools, jobs, neighborhoods, and other amenities.

In contrast, the boundaries separating SCE European immigrants and people of Northern European ancestry were far blurrier. As described in chapter 3, these groups were racialized and treated poorly in the early twentieth century. For example, Italians often were openly discriminated against in hiring and employment advertisements, as well as stereotyped as having criminal tendencies or anarchist sympathies. But as Cybelle Fox and Thomas Guglielmo argue persuasively, they still were classified within the broad category of "white" in the eyes of the law and treated accordingly.[19] For example, even though social distance made marriage between SCE Europeans and Northwest Europeans rare, it was more common than black-white marriages, and it was never illegal. Fox and Guglielmo further note that "in the hundreds of state laws and local ordinances that required racial segregation in schools, streetcars, water fountains, hospitals, and the like, not one of these ever singled out [SCE Europeans] or defined them as non-white."[20] Likewise, even though Americanization programs run by white

Protestants pressured SCE European immigrants to downplay their ethnic identities and practices, no laws prohibited them from participating in local and national politics through naturalizing, or from voting and joining labor unions.

The distinction between discrimination aimed toward European immigrants and that directed toward blacks is very important. As discussed in chapter 2, Charles Hirschman characterizes the former as ethnocentrism and the latter as racism.[21] Ethnocentrism is a commonly held preference for one's own group and antipathy toward outsiders. It holds that if "the outsiders were to give up their foreign ways, they could (and would) become members of our society."[22] In contrast, racism is an ideology that "holds that otherness is not simply a product of socialization, language, or culture, but is part of the inherent character of different groups."[23]

Were the boundaries between Mexican Americans and non-Hispanic whites (also referred to as "Anglos" in some settings) bright or blurry? Did they experience racism akin to that experienced by blacks, or did they contend with a form of ethnocentrism familiar to most SCE European groups? The answer is that it depended on several factors, including where Mexican Americans lived, their socioeconomic status, their skin color, and whether they were in a courtroom versus a social setting.

Mexican Americans were defined as "white" under the law. The Treaty of Guadalupe Hidalgo stipulated that Mexicans living in the territories annexed by the United States in 1848 would be granted the full rights of U.S. citizens: eligibility for naturalization, full voting rights, and access to the same resources as whites. Similarly, intermarriage between Mexicans and Anglos was not against the law. Still, many ordinary Americans did not recognize Mexicans as white, so their treatment and racial classification varied by location and often depended on skin tone or socioeconomic status.

For example, Montejano describes large variations by class in Texas, where Mexican Americans who were educated, spoke English, or owned land commingled and attended school with Anglos and married Anglos, while poor Mexican immigrants (often those with indigenous or *mestizo* [mixed European and indigenous] ancestry) were subject to much the same treatment as blacks.[24] Citing Paul Taylor, a Department of Agriculture economist carrying out fieldwork on Mexican labor in the 1930s, Fox and Guglielmo quote a Texas lawyer: "Our people don't recognize them [Mexicans] as white people," even though "the law does. There is the same race prejudice here as against the Negro."[25]

The confusion about whether Mexicans were white was reflected in the U.S. census. The 1930 census classified Mexicans as a separate race (that is, as not white), but after the Mexican American population and the Mexican government protested, the 1940 census enumerated them as white.[26] As Fox and Guglielmo write, "At some times and places, all Mexicans were white; other times and places they were not. At some times and places, an individual Mexican's personal characteristics—socioeconomic status or skin tone, for example—could make her or him white; other times and places they could not."[27]

The contrast between Texas and California, the top two states of residence for Mexican Americans, was particularly stark. In 1940, 40 percent of Mexican Americans (both U.S.- and foreign-born) lived in Texas and 28 percent lived in California.[28] A large share of newly arrived Mexican male immigrants in both states was employed in agriculture (38 percent in both states) or as some other type of laborer (33 percent in Texas and 39 percent in California). Their treatment in the two states was quite different, and we argue in a manner consistent with Fox that sociological and historical work has largely failed to appropriately highlight the distinctions between these two contexts and how these differences have shaped contemporary patterns of Mexican American integration.

Texas featured a system of structural racism that went beyond individual attitudes or racial slurs. It was embedded in systems, laws, and written or unwritten policies that determined which groups got power and resources. Such a system is sometimes referred to as "institutional racism," because it describes how racism is embedded in social structures. Texas joined the United States as a slave state in 1845, when most Texan Anglos descended from resettled southerners who fought to maintain the "color line" and extend it to Mexicans.[29] Most of the Mexican population in Texas was living in southern Texas and nearby San Antonio with almost no other nonwhites to impede the placement of Mexicans at the bottom of a sharply defined, two-caste racial system.[30] Racial discrimination against Mexicans was so pervasive that Mexico, under the Bracero Program, banned Texas from receiving Mexican workers.[31]

The structural racism directed toward Mexican Americans in Texas was encapsulated in the wage differential between Texas and California. Texas growers in each county kept wages low by fixing the price of labor each season. In 1940, the average Mexican-born male farm laborer in Texas made only half of what a similar worker made in California. The California-Texas wage ratio for farm laborers persisted from 1940 (the earliest year we could find data) until about 1980. In 1940, Mexican farm laborers made $2.10 in California for every dollar earned in Texas. Although housing prices were lower in Texas than California, rent and other living expenses were about the same in the two states.[32]

Texan employers were able to keep wages low because they constructed a "web of labor controls" to discourage Mexican employees from seeking better-paying work elsewhere.[33] Sharecroppers and tenant farmers could be immobilized through a perpetual cycle of debt, particularly when they were forced to purchase goods on credit from a company store. Vagrancy laws and pass systems also were used to restrict the movement of seasonal farm workers. For example, in a scheme discovered in one Texas county, labor recruiters would convince Mexicans to agree to work on false pretenses, only to change the terms of employment after they started work. If a worker quit, the local sheriff would pick them up on vagrancy laws. Unable to pay the fines, the workers were forced to work under the conditions and for the employer they had just rejected. It also was common for employers to dismiss seasonal workers at the end of the season without full payment by way of threats (for example, "shotgun settlements") or timely leaks to the border patrol.

Mexicans were further hindered by efforts to prevent them from driving. Montejano notes, "Large landowners were expressly against the 'good roads' program and ownership of cars by Mexican laborers."[34] In Texas, roads were rarely paved in Mexican towns, and employers were reluctant to hire Mexicans who owned cars. Mexicans leaving the state would need to be on constant watch for patrolmen as well as agents of the Texas Farm Placement Service or the Texas Bureau of Motor Carriers: "Thus, Mexican truck drivers, loaded with their cargo of Mexican laborers, usually drove at night, through back roads, following a zig-zag course to the beet fields of Michigan."[35]

The system of labor controls in Texas extended to schools. We describe the schooling situation in greater detail in chapter 5; here it is important to know that there was little interest among those in power in providing educational opportunities to Mexican American children in Texas. Schooling kept older children out of the labor force and could lead them to seek middle-class occupations. As Montejano notes, "The key element in Mexican school policy was the concern of farmers in securing and controlling farm labor. If farmers were to keep this labor reservoir, Mexicans had to be kept ignorant."[36] Starting in 1915, Texas required children to attend school between the ages of eight and fifteen, but this law was rarely enforced for Mexican children.[37] Moreover, in circumstances in which Mexican children attended school, they were usually sent to underfunded schools that were separate from Anglo schools. Although Mexican children were counted in the funding formulas for public schools, school boards often spent most of those funds on "American" schools while state officials overlooked the illegality of this practice. Another Texas school administrator, noting the failures of the school system for Mexicans, admitted, "It isn't a matter of what is the best way to handle the education here to make citizens of them. It is politics. . . . The farmers are not interested in educating the Mexicans. They know that then they can get better wages and conditions."[38]

Montejano points out cracks in the system that limited the extent to which employers could exploit Mexican labor. For example, some Mexicans did manage to leave the state, and Mexican Americans in Texas were known to boycott stores or employers in protest of particularly repressive laws or practices. Still, even the Mexican American social movements in Texas needed to bend to the deeply entrenched racial hierarchy there. Rather than seeking to dismantle racial discrimination, they distanced themselves from African Americans and defined themselves as white to gain rights and privileges.[39]

California was not immune to racism, but Mexicans there were less likely to be suppressed under a coordinated system of structural racism than in Texas. In contrast to the rest of the United States, nineteenth-century California had sizable numbers of Asians, blacks, Mexicans, and Native Americans who, though racialized in relation to one another, were all beneath whites in the racial hierarchy.[40] To be sure, there was discrimination against Mexicans in California.[41] This was evident, for example, from the repatriation campaigns of the 1930s and the "Zoot Suit Riots" in 1943.[42] Still, Anglos perceived less social distance between themselves and Mexicans than they did with other nonwhite groups, given that Mexicans practiced Christianity, had Spanish ancestry, spoke a Romance language, and had European features.[43]

Another important difference between California and Texas is that California entered the union as a free, nonslavery state in 1850 and therefore did not attract people with vested interests in slavery or near-slavery forms of labor control. As described in George Sanchez's account of Mexican Americans in Los Angeles, Southern California attracted Protestant midwesterners in the early 1900s, many of whom were accustomed to and engaged in efforts to "Americanize" immigrants.[44] Mirroring the Americanization programs developed in the Northeast and Midwest, they first attempted to acculturate Mexican immigrant men. After discovering that the men were too busy working to take classes in English, civics, and American culture, they shifted their attention to Mexican immigrant women and their children. Americanization classes took place in Mexican American homes and involved instruction in English, cooking, cleaning, and even personal appearance, often with the goal of making Mexican American women more suitable for domestic service jobs in Anglo homes and Americanizing their children.

The degree to which Mexican Americans in California were expected to give up their ethnic identity varied over time. After Hiram Johnson was elected governor of California in 1910, he promoted Americanization policies that recognized the unique contributions of ethnic groups. In 1913, Governor Johnson established the Commission of Immigration and Housing (CIH), which aimed to promote the integration and socioeconomic mobility of the state's growing immigrant population. Simon Lupin, who eventually led the CIH, wrote that he "envisioned an agency which would promote mutual accommodation between the native-born and foreign-born, with a focus on 'immigrant gifts'—the cultural strengths that foreigners brought with them to American society."[45] Later in the 1910s, as World War I heightened anxieties about foreigners, Governor Johnson's progressive policies lost support. The CIH was eventually dismantled in 1923 under conservative governor Friend Richardson. The pendulum swung back in the 1930s and 1940s, however, owing to mobilization efforts among the Mexican American community in California. Organizations such as the Congress of Spanish Speaking Peoples, formed in 1938, denounced racial discrimination and emphasized a Chicano identity—in remarkable contrast to the social movements in Texas.[46]

Educational expenditure data illustrate how much California stood out from other states in its intensive efforts to incorporate immigrants through its educational programs. During the 1920s and 1930s, night schools taught immigrants the English language and culture and gave them vocational training. As shown in figure 4.1, night school expenditures per 1,000 people in 1930 were the highest in California and the Northeast (for example, in New York, New Jersey, Connecticut, and Massachusetts).

Census statistics also illustrate the vast differences between California and Texas in the educational opportunities of Mexican Americans. For example, as late as 1960 the median years of schooling among Spanish-surname adults in Texas was just 4.8 years, compared to 8.6 in California, 7.0 in Arizona, 8.2 in Colorado, and 7.4 in New Mexico.[47] The gap in years of schooling between Spanish-surname adults and Anglos in Texas was 6.7 years, compared to 3.6 years in California.[48] These statistics do not differentiate by generational status, but they do suggest a close correlation between the structural racism in Texas and Mexican Americans' educational opportunities in that state.

The stark differences between California and Texas in terms of how educators and educational institutions approached the schooling of non-white and immigrant-origin children are also reflected in the reports of the respective state superintendents of public instruction. For example, large sections of California's state superintendent reports from the 1920s focus on in-depth and expansive discussions of the state's efforts to successfully integrate the children of immigrant families into the school system and develop the best practices to ensure their scholastic success. These passages also devote considerable attention to efforts to provide a robust system of night school education to immigrant adults; in total, these reports reflect a broad-based and institutionalized effort to promote the educational success of immigrant children in California. In contrast, the Texas superintendent reports from the same period are notable for the absence of discussion of the educational disadvantages faced by immigrant and minority populations.[49]

Overall, the racial boundaries between Mexicans and Anglos during the first three decades of the twentieth century were brighter in Texas than they were in California. The lines dividing Mexicans from Anglos in Texas were enforced through coordinated actions by employers, law enforcement officers, judges, superintendents, and state officials. Although there were cracks in the system that Mexicans were able to exploit, their opportunities

Figure 4.1 *Night School Expenditures per 1,000 People, 1930*

$286

$0

Source: Data from the Biennial Survey of Education.

for upward mobility were deliberately constrained by a system of structural racism akin to the Jim Crow legal systems used to suppress African Americans. In contrast, the racial boundaries between Mexicans and Anglos in California were blurrier. The Americanization policies directed toward Mexicans, though ethnocentric, sought to incorporate rather than exclude, and at times they allowed for the retention or development of Chicano identities.

Educational Attainment

To analyze the educational attainment of early-vintage Mexican Americans to see how their progress across generations compared with that of other groups living in the country at the time, we again drew on the IGENS-20 linked data described in chapter 2 and employed in the analysis for European-origin groups in chapter 3. All the families in our sample could trace their immigrant origins to their parents or grandparents who were living in the country and were enumerated in the 1940 census.

As detailed in chapter 2, we compared Mexican American families with three other groups: native white families, native black families, and Italian American families. Native whites—defined in the IGENS-20 data as families headed by U.S.-born white parents—are an important comparison group because they represented the American mainstream during the early and middle parts of the twentieth century. They constituted the majority group that typically occupied the highest socioeconomic and political positions and were the least likely to experience discrimination on account of race or ethnicity.

In contrast, native blacks were treated as second-class citizens with fewer legal rights. They did not have equal access to education, housing, or jobs, they endured especially harsh treatment in the South, and they continue to have some of the lowest educational attainments of all U.S. racial and ethnic groups today. Determining whether early-vintage immigrants' outcomes matched those of their contemporary native white or black peers is crucial for gauging the degree to which they were being racialized as a low-status group. Groups that matched or exceeded the outcomes of native whites can be thought of as eventually being integrated into the American mainstream, whereas groups attaining outcomes like those of native blacks were more likely to encounter longer-lasting barriers to upward mobility.

Finally, Italian Americans are an important comparison group because they were similar in many ways to Mexican Americans, including their labor migration experiences, rural peasant origins, discriminatory treatment in the labor force, and strong reliance on family and the Catholic Church for support.[50] As observed in the previous chapter, Italian Americans set the standard for how far a low-status immigrant group could go in mid-twentieth-century America if given the chance.

Generational Change in Educational Attainment

Educational attainment was low among both Mexican and Italian immigrants. In 1940, Mexican immigrants had an average of 3.8 years of schooling and Italian immigrants had only 4.6 years. Both groups had lower educational attainment than native blacks (5.5 years) and native whites (8.7 years). However, schooling increased across generations for all groups, as did the percentages of students who completed high school or four years of college. For example, among native white families, educational attainment increased to 12.5 years for their children (the second generation) and 14.0 years for their grandchildren (the third generation).

As transformative as these increases in education have been for American society, our primary interest lies in the degree to which Mexican Americans and other low-status groups fell behind (or caught up to) native whites across generations. In figure 4.2, therefore, we show the *relative* advantages or disadvantages of each group compared with their native white peers. Lines that fall below the horizontal axis indicate that the group has lower educational attainment than native whites, and lines that extend above the axis signify a higher attainment. This chart makes it easy to see

Figure 4.2 *Gaps in Educational Attainment between Early-Vintage Mexican Americans, Italian Americans, and Native Blacks and Whites, by Generational Status*

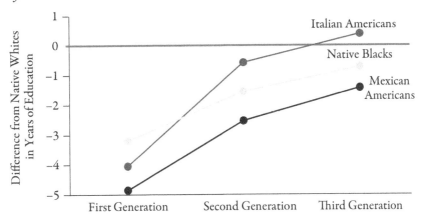

Source: Analysis based on the IGENS-20 linked data files.

Notes: The sample includes Mexican American, Italian American, and native black and white adults ages twenty-five and older from the early vintage. The Census Bureau's disclosure review board and disclosure avoidance officers have reviewed this information product for unauthorized disclosure of confidential information and approved the disclosure avoidance practices applied to this release. This research was performed at a federal statistical research data center under FSRDC Project 2357 (CBDRB-FY22-P2357-R9408).

how the relative advantages and disadvantages for each group changed across generations.

Even though the gaps in years of schooling between native whites and the other groups narrowed across generations, Mexican Americans remained the most disadvantaged group throughout the eight-decade period. In 1940, Mexicans lagged behind whites by 4.9 years. This gap was reduced to 2.5 years for the second generation and 1.4 years for the third. In contrast, Italian Americans experienced rapid upward mobility, nearly matching native whites' educational levels by the second generation and exceeding them by the third. This same pattern was shown in chapter 3 for all Southern Europeans—a group composed of Italians as well as Greeks, Spaniards, and others.

These patterns are also evident when we examine the share of those who completed high school, at least some postsecondary schooling, and college. High school completion rates among all groups increased with each new generation. For example, the share of Mexican Americans completing high school increased across generations from 4.6 percent (first generation) to 50.7 percent (second generation) to 80.5 percent (third generation). Likewise, the share of Mexican Americans completing college increased from 0.8 percent to 8.3 percent to 16.5 percent.

However, as shown in figure 4.3, group disparities grew across generations, particularly in the share completing at least some postsecondary schooling and the share completing a four-year college degree. In 1940, all three groups—Italians, Mexicans, and native blacks—completed high school, attained at least some postsecondary schooling, and completed college at about the same rate, and all three groups had lower attainment rates than native whites. However, Italian Americans nearly closed the gap with whites in high school completion by the second generation, and they exceeded whites for all three educational milestones by the third.

In contrast, both native blacks and Mexican Americans fell further behind in high school completion in the second generation and did not start to close their respective gaps vis-à-vis native whites until the third generation. Even more worrisome, native blacks and Mexican American disadvantages in college completion grew steadily across generations. For example, among those in the first generation, the percentage of Mexican Americans who completed college was 2.6 percentage points lower than the percentage for whites. By the second generation, this disadvantage grew to 11.6 percentage points. By the third generation, it was 19.6 percentage points. College completion rates increased for all groups with each new generation, but the rates were slower among Mexican Americans. Both they and native blacks fell further and further behind.

Part of the reason for the low attainments for Mexican Americans and native blacks is that they started with such low educational attainment in 1940. However, this is not the complete story. Italian immigrants also had low levels of education in 1940 (falling between native blacks and Mexican immigrants) but were able to catch up with and even surpass whites by the third generation. Mexican Americans and blacks, on the other hand, were less upwardly mobile than Italian Americans during the middle of the twentieth century, even after accounting for their parents' educational attainment.[51]

Legacy Effects

The low starting points of the Mexican first generation and the second generation's slow mobility are not just interesting historical facts. They are important for understanding contemporary inequality. The connections between parents' and children's adult statuses are strong in the United States. Parents' and even grandparents' education are associated with income, wealth, and access to better neighborhoods and school systems, and these resources shape children's schooling experiences and their ability to finish

Figure 4.3 *Gaps in High School Completion, Some Postsecondary Attainment, and College Completion between Early-Vintage Mexican Americans, Italian Americans, and Native Blacks and Whites, by Generational Status*

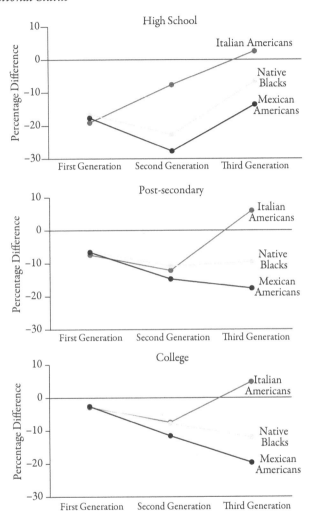

Source: Analysis based on the IGENS-20 linked data files.
Notes: The sample includes Mexican American, Italian American, and native black and white adults ages twenty-five and older from the early vintage. The Census Bureau's disclosure review board and disclosure avoidance officers have reviewed this information product for unauthorized disclosure of confidential information and approved the disclosure avoidance practices applied to this release. This research was performed at a federal statistical research data center under FSRDC Project 2357 (CBDRB-FY22-P2357-R9408).

high school and college.[52] The disadvantages Mexican Americans experienced during the 1930s and 1940s have been transmitted to the third generation today.

To gauge the strength of these legacy effects, we simulated how much of the disadvantage for third-generation Mexican Americans is attributable to the disadvantages of their grandparents and parents by developing a three-generation mobility model for each origin group. This model, illustrated in figure 4.4, is an equation that articulates the mathematical relationship between a group's educational distribution in the third generation (D), the group's educational distribution in the first generation (A), and the degree of intergenerational mobility between the first and second generations (B) and the second and third generations (C). We provide computational details for interested readers in online supplement 4.3.

After estimating empirical inputs for each component of the model for each group (as observed in reality), we changed the inputs to simulate an alternative reality. First, we assigned first-generation Mexicans the same educational attainment as native whites in 1940. Second, we assigned Mexican immigrant families the same rates of intergenerational mobility between the first and second generations as for native whites. Third, we assigned Mexicans and native whites the same rates of intergenerational mobility between the second and third generations. In each of these scenarios, we examined how the change in inputs affected Mexican American third-generation educational attainment. These results reveal how much of the disadvantage in educational attainment for third-generation Mexican Americans compared with native whites is due to lower educational attainment in the first generation, lower mobility between the first and second generations, and lower mobility between the second and third generations.

The results are shown in figure 4.5. They indicate that between 60 and

Figure 4.4 *Three-Generation Mobility Model*

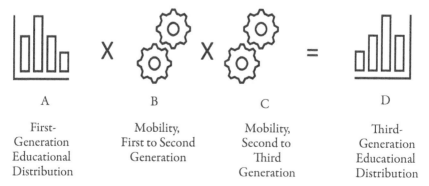

	First-Generation Educational Distribution		Mobility, First to Second Generation		Mobility, Second to Third Generation		Third-Generation Educational Distribution
	A		B		C		D

Source: Authors' construction.

Figure 4.5 *Gaps in Schooling between Third-Generation Mexican Americans and Native Whites Associated with Differences in First-Generation Attainment and Intergenerational Mobility for Subsequent Generations, Adults Ages Twenty-Five and Older, Early Vintage*

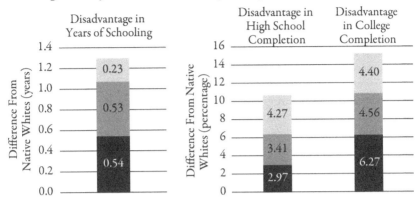

▨ Due to Lower Intergenerational Mobility for Third Generation
▩ Due to Lower Intergenerational Mobility for Second Generation
■ Due to Lower Attainment of First Generation

Source: IGENS-20 linked data files.
Notes: Any views expressed are those of the authors and not those of the U.S. Census Bureau. The Census Bureau's disclosure review board and disclosure avoidance officers have reviewed this information product for unauthorized disclosure of confidential information and approved the disclosure avoidance practices applied to this release. This research was performed at a federal statistical research data center under FSRDC Project 2357 (CBDRB-FY22-P2357-R9408).

80 percent of contemporary inequality in educational attainment between Mexican Americans and native whites can be traced back to the low attainments and limited opportunities of earlier generations. Third-generation Mexican Americans have about 1.3 fewer years of schooling than native whites, but 42 percent of this difference (0.54 years) is due to the low educational attainment of first-generation Mexican immigrants who arrived during the Industrial Era, and another 40 percent (0.50 years) is due to the low rates of upward mobility between the first and second generations. We found similar patterns when we looked at key educational milestones. Large shares of Mexicans' disadvantages in high school (60 percent) and college completion (80 percent) are attributable to these historical factors.

To think about how this process may have played out, consider the typical early-vintage Mexican American family. Back in the 1950s and 1960s, few were able to take advantage of the post–World War II expansion in public education. While most people back then managed to get a high school diploma, which was freely available to all children, Mexican Americans were an exception. Only half of second-generation Mexican Americans attained a high school diploma. Without this increasingly important credential, they missed other opportunities later in life. For example, few were able to attain good jobs with decent pay in the rapidly expanding postwar economy. Our data show that second-generation Mexican men of working age made 84 cents for every dollar earned by native white men. Additionally, they were less likely—by 10 percentage points—to have a professional or managerial job. By comparison, second-generation Southern Europeans made $1.14 for every dollar earned by native white men and were much more likely—by 13 percentage points—to have a professional or managerial job.

Those lost opportunities reduced their third-generation children's chances for upward mobility. Low education, poverty, and residence in areas with underfunded schools may have made it difficult for second-generation Mexican American parents to launch their third-generation children into college and beyond. Instead of being supported by their parents, their children may have felt pressure to contribute to their family's finances by working rather than going to college, a common pattern among Mexican American families that has been noted by several observers.[53] Adding to their difficulties, the cost of higher education started to rise faster than inflation in the 1980s and 1990s, making it even more difficult for Mexican American families to finance their children's education. For example, in 1968, the registration fee for all students was $300 per year at campuses in the University of California system, and tuition was free to all California residents.[54] In-state tuition and fees were $1,296 in 1985, $7,434 in 2004, and $14,500 in 2021.[55] A report by the Public Policy Institute of California found that tuition and fees in the University of California system have increased by an average of 8.6 percent annually since 1979—more than double the 3.1 percent annual increase in inflation.[56] Still, the third generation does appear to have taken advantage of lower-cost educational opportunities. The fact that they attend community colleges and technical schools at higher rates than their native white peers suggests that if higher education were made more affordable, some of the disadvantages for third-generation Mexican Americans would diminish. For now, barriers to higher education, especially the more expensive options (four-year colleges), remain.

Structural Racism and Place of Residence

The idea that the United States provides a level playing field is a powerful American belief. It undergirds the trope that success is a well-deserved reward for hard work.[57] However, the contrast in the experiences of Italian Americans and those of Mexican Americans calls into question the existence of the level playing field. Given that Mexican and Italian immigrants started their lives in the United States with the same levels of education, what does it say about our country that the offspring of one group did phenomenally well while the offspring of the other group struggled?

As we discussed in the previous chapter, some observers no doubt would point to the attributes of the groups themselves to explain why this happened. They might argue that there must be something special about the Italians that propelled them upward, or something lacking in Mexicans that held them back. Such arguments no doubt underlie the concerns that some have about the declining "quality" of newly arrived U.S. immigrants, especially those coming from Mexico and Central America.[58] As is evident in Cybelle Fox's analysis of discriminatory laws directed toward Mexican immigrants in the early twentieth century, it is clear that Mexicans were treated differently than Italians.[59]

Furthermore, there has been tremendous variation in outcomes *among* Mexican Americans depending on where they lived. As discussed in chapter 2, social scientists theorize that inequality in immigrant integration is closely tied to the degree to which institutions create and reinforce racial hierarchies, such as in Texas when superintendents, sheriffs, and growers colluded to keep Mexican American wages low and discourage Mexican American children from attending school. If such treatment is the root cause of Mexican Americans' poor outcomes, then we should see the slowest integration among those who grew up in times and places with the greatest levels of structural racism, such as in Texas during the early twentieth century. Where and when structural racism against Mexican Americans was less entrenched, such as in California, the Midwest, and the Northeast, we should see patterns of integration for Mexican Americans more like those seen among Italian Americans.

This is exactly what we find.

In 1940, Italian and Mexican immigrants lived in different parts of the country. This is shown in the map in figure 4.6. Most Italian immigrants—nearly 90 percent—lived in the Northeast (72 percent) or the Midwest (15 percent), and 65 percent were concentrated in one of four states: New York, New Jersey, Pennsylvania, and Massachusetts. In contrast, 90 percent of Mexican immigrants lived either in the southern (40 percent) or western (50 percent) regions of the United States, with 39 percent in Texas and 36 percent in California. Place of residence was not strongly associated with upward mobility among Italian Americans, and the generational patterns of European-origin immigrants, including Southern Europeans, were similar across U.S. regions.[60] Our data reveal this same pattern for Italians. However, place of residence was much more consequential for Mexican Americans.

Figure 4.6 *Distribution of Italian and Mexican Immigrants across States, 1940*

Mexican Immigrants

Italian Immigrants

Source: Ruggles et al. 2024.
Notes: Fewer than 6 percent of Mexican immigrants resided in the thirty-eight states without labels combined. Fewer than 6 percent of Italian immigrants resided in the thirty-three states without labels combined.

First, we found that Mexican American children were much more likely to attend school when their families moved away from Texas. Of course, it is possible that those who left the state did so because they wanted better opportunities for themselves and their children. Because of their high aspirations, their children might have gone further in school no matter where they lived, even if they stayed in Texas. In other words, what might appear to be a *place effect* could instead be a *family effect.* However, we were able to isolate *place* effects by following the same families over time as they moved from place to place by using a publicly available dataset consisting of linked 1930 and 1940 census records (described in greater detail in section 2.1 of the online supplement). We focused on whether adolescent children ages twelve to eighteen were enrolled in school, because middle school and high school attendance is a very good indicator of a person's educational attainment in adulthood. We looked at how this indicator changed for Mexican American families before and after they moved to or from Texas. In general, attendance rates increased over time, but the amount it increased varied a lot depending on where they lived. Among parents who lived in Texas in 1930, enrollment rates for their adolescent children in 1940 were on average twenty-one percentage points higher if they moved to California than if they remained in Texas. Conversely, among Mexican American parents who lived in California in 1930, enrollment rates for their children in 1940 were eleven percentage points higher if they remained in California than if they moved to Texas. Finally, the enrollment rates of children in states other than California or Texas in 1930 were highest if they moved to California and lowest if they moved to Texas. In other words, moving to Texas or staying in Texas was not conducive to Mexican American children's schooling.[61]

Second, we examined the completed educational attainment for second-generation Mexican Americans who grew up in any of the ten most populous states for Mexican immigrants in 1940; 93 percent of Mexican immigrants lived in one of these states in 1940. We charted Mexican Americans' average years of schooling, expressed as the difference from native whites in the same state (dots in figure 4.7). We also included data on second-generation Italian Americans as a point of comparison (triangles in figure 4.7). Among Italian Americans, educational attainment did not vary much by state; it hovered at or just below the level of native whites in all ten states. Mexican Americans, however, fell behind both native whites and Italian Americans. By far, their disadvantage relative to native whites was the greatest in Texas (about four years), moderate in western states (about two and a half years), and smallest in the Midwest, especially Illinois, Michigan, Ohio, and Indiana (between one and two years).

Finally, we examined upward mobility—the extent to which second-generation children went beyond their parents in school—separately by region. Our sample was too small to examine mobility separately by state,

Figure 4.7 Gaps in Educational Attainment between Early-Vintage Native Whites and Second-Generation Mexican Americans and Italian Americans, 1920–1940 Birth Cohorts, by State

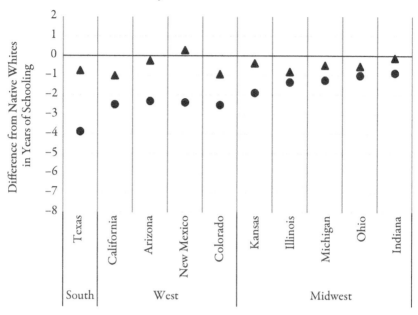

● Mexican American   ▲ Italian American

Source: Analysis based on the IGENS-20 linked data files.
Notes: The sample includes second-generation European-born and native white adults ages twenty-five and older in the early vintage. Differences are adjusted for parents' education, family structure, number of siblings, year of birth, and gender. Any views expressed are those of the authors and not those of the U.S. Census Bureau. The Census Bureau's disclosure review board and disclosure avoidance officers have reviewed this information product for unauthorized disclosure of confidential information and approved the disclosure avoidance practices applied to this release. This research was performed at a federal statistical research data center under FSRDC Project 2357 (CBDRB-FY22-P2357-R9503).

but it is important to recognize that nearly all Mexican Americans living in the South at this time were living in Texas (98 percent). We found that upward mobility was slower among Mexican Americans in the South (Texas) than in other regions.[62] Mexican American children in the Midwest or Northeast did just as well as whites with the same parental education. In the South (Texas), second-generation Mexican Americans were much more disadvantaged. They had 1.4 fewer years of schooling than their native white peers with the same parental education. Second-generation Mexican Americans who grew up in the West fell in the middle. They had 0.7 fewer years of schooling than their native white peers.

Overall, when we consider the historical record of structural racism directed toward Mexicans in Texas, it is clear that the system designed to subjugate early-vintage Mexican Americans slowed their educational mobility. The statistical evidence we compiled corroborates this account. Second-generation Mexican Americans would have had higher levels of middle and high school enrollment, smaller disadvantages in completed education relative to native whites, and greater intergenerational mobility had they not remained or lived in Texas.

Summary

Mexicans started migrating to the United States in large numbers at the beginning of the twentieth century. Like other Industrial Era immigrants, they tended to arrive with low levels of education and worked low-skilled jobs in agriculture and manufacturing. Their similarities with Italian immigrants are especially notable. Both groups were low-skilled labor migrants with strong familial ties and Catholic affiliations, and both experienced discrimination in the labor force.

Despite the similarities between Italians and Mexicans, their social mobility paths in the United States diverged quickly. Early-vintage, Industrial Era Mexicans did not experience the same treatment, particularly in racist contexts like Jim Crow Texas, nor did they have the same outcomes as Italians, resulting in a pattern of slow and incomplete integration. First, their educational attainments were low. Among the first, second, and even third generation, their attainments were the lowest of all the ethnoracial groups we examined, including native blacks and Italian Americans. Second, they experienced the slowest intergenerational mobility between the first and second generations (that is, during the 1940s, 1950s, and 1960s) of all the groups we examined. Third, their historical disadvantages, including their low starting points in the first generation and low mobility between the first and second generations, explain between 60 and 80 percent of the educational disadvantages seen among third-generation Mexican Americans today.

In short, our comparison of these two early-vintage immigrant groups illuminates the legacy of racist contexts of reception for early-vintage Mexican immigrants and their children. They were not integrated as Italians were, and they did not experience the same degree of success as Italians. These historical disadvantages were passed on to their children and grandchildren.

Finally, Mexican Americans' outcomes differed from those of Italians because they experienced a particularly pernicious type of discrimination that emphasized permanent exclusion and subjugation as low-wage laborers, especially in Texas. Perhaps the most telling finding presented in this chapter is that second-generation Mexican American children did better if they lived in California, and nearly as well as Italian Americans when they lived in or moved to midwestern states, such as Illinois, Michigan, Ohio, or Indiana. During the early twentieth century, more Mexican Americans lived in Texas than in any other state, and only a minority lived in the Midwest. The relative success of those living outside of Texas is a sad indicator of the lost opportunities, *of what could have been*, had Mexican Americans been treated more fairly in Texas.

~ Chapter 5 ~

The Leveling Effects of Industrial Era School Expansion

Through the establishment of industrial standards we propose to secure to the able-bodied immigrant and to his native fellow workers a larger share of American opportunity. We denounce the fatal policy of indifference and neglect which has left our enormous immigrant population to become the prey of chance and cupidity. We favor Governmental action to encourage the distribution of immigrants away from the congested cities, to rigidly supervise all private agencies dealing with them and to promote their assimilation, education and advancement.

—"A Contract with the People: Platform of the Progressive Party Adopted at Its First National Convention," Progressive National Committee, 1912, 15

The board won't let me enforce compulsory attendance. . . . If I tried to enforce [it] the board would get sore at me. . . . If I got 150 Mexicans ready for school I would be out of a job.

—School superintendent near Corpus Christi, Texas, early 1930s, quoted in Paul Taylor, *An American-Mexican Frontier*, 1934, 194–97

The diverging mobility patterns presented in the preceding chapters, between early-vintage Europeans and their Mexican American peers, raise a question that has long vexed American social scientists: Why did these patterns diverge? During an era in which the federal government was so active through policy and investment in increasing the human capital and prosperity of average Americans, why did the benefits accrue so disproportionately to some marginalized populations (Italians) while failing to benefit others (native blacks and Mexican Americans) to a similar degree?

https://doi.org/10.7758/fhka5464.2755

Of course, given the long struggle with race relations growing out of the nation's institutionalization of slavery and confinement of surviving indigenous populations to reservations, the obvious answer to this question is that such inequalities derive from race prejudice and discrimination and the institutionalization of these dynamics in a racially unequal opportunity structure. As the common explanation goes, unlike the ethnoracial groups that were largely excluded from expanding Industrial Era and midcentury mobility opportunities, the European immigrant groups were defined as racially white. In this view, race and racial boundaries explain these divergent group outcomes.

However, more specific answers are needed to avoid the mistakes of the past and improve future outcomes for immigrant children. How exactly was prejudice and discrimination institutionalized? Can prejudice be deinstitutionalized so that all children have opportunities? As we showed in the last chapter, the disadvantages for Mexican Americans were particularly glaring in Texas. Educational outcomes, like children's school attendance and adult educational attainment, were better and much more similar to those of Italians and non-Hispanic whites among the Mexican American families who left Texas and moved to places like Michigan, Illinois, and California. What was special about these places that helped equalize outcomes, and could their policies be successfully applied elsewhere?

The contrasting epigraphs at the start of this chapter—one from the American Progressive Party promoting immigrant education, the other from a Texas school superintendent explaining why he didn't enforce compulsory school attendance laws for Mexicans—point us clearly in the direction of schools. The American system of public schooling is commonly perceived to be a "leveling" institution. That is, in accordance with the principle of equal access to opportunity, the public education system aims to provide the requisite training and knowledge for the pursuit of occupational and economic opportunity to all Americans regardless of their social class or ethnoracial identity. In other words, public schooling ideally aims to erase the disadvantages of family background in order to provide all children with equal footing on which to succeed.

The opportunities opened up by public education are of crucial importance for the children of immigrant groups whose parents faced huge disadvantages in human capital relative to other groups. During the Industrial Era, the development and resources of school systems—and thus their "leveling capacity"—varied tremendously across states and regions. A child's ability to take advantage of educational opportunities depended on where their parents settled. How important were these variations in educational opportunity for producing the disadvantages in educational attainment we see today among early-vintage Mexican Americans? As we show in this chapter, they were crucial.

Ethnocentric versus Racialized Schooling Contexts

The end of the nineteenth century and the first half of the twentieth saw a remarkable expansion of American public schooling.[1] However, in crucial respects this expansion unfolded very unevenly across the United States. The Northeast and Midwest, especially in the urban industrial centers where the new European immigrants were concentrated, stood at the forefront of this expansion. The school bureaucracies in the South, which had been designed to maintain racially separate systems of education, were slow to modernize, and the expansion of public schooling there lagged behind other parts of the country by several decades.[2] To consider the implications of this variation in Industrial Era school contexts for immigrant integration, we return to Hirschman's conceptual distinction between ethnocentrism and racism, discussed in detail in chapter 2. In some places—particularly in the Northeast, Midwest, California, and places like Grand Rapids, Michigan, where Jenny's grandparents attended school, and New York City, where the Baldizzi family lived—the Progressive Era program of "Americanization" was highly influential. Americanization efforts were also prevalent in the Upper Midwest, where Jim's German-Russian ancestors put down roots.[3] We see these places as providing "ethnocentric schooling contexts." The Progressive and Americanization movements had little social and political influence in other places, such as in Texas and other parts of the South. We see the educational systems in those places as providing "racialized schooling contexts."

Though the Americanization efforts in Progressive Era schools viewed civic integration as conditional on acculturation—or the adoption of American cultural norms and beliefs—the overarching goal in these contexts was integration in the form of universal day school attendance. As state educational bureaucracies developed in Progressive school contexts, enforcing attendance and providing a uniform instructional experience became administrative objectives in and of themselves. Over time, the bureaucratic objectives of state agencies superseded those of local elites whose economic interests may have been better served by keeping poor and minority children out of school and in the workforce. Even if cast in ethnocentric terms, the motivating logic, captured in the quote from the Progressive Party platform at the opening of the chapter, is integration. In ethnocentric schooling contexts, racial (or class) boundaries are blurred, and because the state works to ensure equal access to schooling, preexisting disadvantages among children that might otherwise produce diverging enrollment and attainment patterns are leveled.

Racialized schooling contexts stand in stark contrast to any leveling processes unfolding in ethnocentric Americanization contexts in that the underlying logic of Jim Crow school systems was the preservation of local whites' political and economic power. This is clearly captured in the sentiment of the 1930s-era Texas school superintendent quoted at the opening of the chapter. By their very design, racialized schooling contexts reinforce existing social inequalities in the provision of educational opportunity, thus locking into place an intergenerational pattern of inequality in access to schooling and educational attainment. The animating philosophy of such contexts is "zero-sum," insofar as affording poor and minority populations opportunities for advancement is assumed to be costly to those in power.

The early twentieth-century Americanization movement played a central role in the development of ethnocentric schooling contexts. The goal of the Americanization movement was to unify a diverse and sprawling national community at a time of great social turbulence that also included urbanization and world war. Progressives and adherents of Americanization viewed the school as a primary locus of Americanizing—a place where children of diverse ethnoracial backgrounds might be bound together in national unity through the provision of a free, common program of formal education. Though cast in ethnocentric terms that most Americans would find objectionable today—insofar as "Americanization" implies a superiority of American culture over others—the goal of the Progressive movement and the Americanization program was to enroll as many children in school as possible, regardless of their background.

Areas of the country where Americanization programs were popular and influential also tended to be places with relatively large numbers of newly arrived Industrial Era immigrants. However, it is likely that educational opportunities would have expanded more rapidly in these locations even without Industrial Era immigration. States like Massachusetts, New York, Michigan, and California boasted well-resourced educational bureaucracies that were relatively well established before mass Industrial Era immigration.

Sociologist John G. Richardson and other experts on the development of the American school system argue that the passage of a compulsory school attendance law marked the "birth" of a state's formal educational bureaucracy.[4] Newborn educational agencies must undergo an early period of development before they grow, establish bureaucratic processes, and command resources.[5] As shown in table 5.1, from 1920 to 1940, the period when the children marking the starting point of our study were born, the age of state school systems varied enormously across the country. In the Northeast, most states had compulsory attendance laws in place by around the time of the Civil War—well prior to the large wave of Industrial Era European migration from 1880 to 1920. Most midwestern and western states adopted their compulsory attendance laws in the first decade of Industrial Era migration and thus lagged behind the Northeast in school system development by about a decade.

The system that eventually grew into a relatively uniform program of public schooling nationwide was built upon the common school system

Table 5.1 *Year in Which Forty-Eight U.S. States and the District of Columbia First Passed Compulsory School Attendance Legislation, by U.S. Region*

The West
Median Enactment Year: 1883
Mean National Rank: 18.2

State	Year	National Rank
Washington	1871	7
New Mexico	1872	8
Nevada	1873	10
California	1874	11
Wyoming	1876	15
Montana	1883	18
Idaho	1887	24
Colorado	1889	26
Oregon	1889	26
Utah	1890	28
Arizona	1899	33

The Midwest
Median Enactment Year: 1883
Mean National Rank: 20.9

State	Year	National Rank
Michigan	1871	5
Kansas	1874	11
Ohio	1877	16
Wisconsin	1879	17
Illinois	1883	18
North Dakota	1883	18
South Dakota	1883	18
Minnesota	1885	23
Nebraska	1887	24
Indiana	1897	31
Iowa	1902	34
Missouri	1905	36

The Northeast
Median Enactment Year: 1872
Mean National Rank: 11.0

State	Year	National Rank
Massachusetts	1852	1
New York	1853	2
Vermont	1867	4
New Hampshire	1871	5
Connecticut	1872	8
Maine	1875	13
New Jersey	1875	13
Rhode Island	1883	18
Pennsylvania	1895	30

The South
Median Enactment Year: 1908
Mean National Rank: 38.0

State	Year	National Rank
District of Columbia	1864	3
Kentucky	1893	29
West Virginia	1897	31
Maryland	1902	34
Tennessee	1905	36
Delaware	1907	38
North Carolina	1907	38
Oklahoma	1907	38
Virginia	1908	41
Arkansas	1909	42
Alabama	1915	43
Florida	1915	43
South Carolina	1915	43
Texas	1915	43
Louisiana	1916	47
Georgia	1916	47
Mississippi	1918	49

Source: Adapted from data in Richardson 1984, table 1.

that already had been established in the colonial states Massachusetts and New York. The educational and other institutions that developed in these states were not formed with the explicit goal of racial exclusion, as they were in former slave states in the South. The institutionalization of racial exclusion in northern states developed somewhat later, coinciding with the Great Migration of black Americans out of the South, starting in the 1920s. The primary mechanism of such exclusion was implemented in the residential housing market rather than in the distribution of educational opportunities per se.[6]

The spirit of the Progressive and Americanization movements ran into an overwhelming oppositional force of institutionalized racial exclusion in the Jim Crow South, where racialized schooling contexts prevailed. Compulsory schooling laws were passed in the Jim Crow South, but it was not uncommon for such mandates to go ignored for decades after enactment as this region continued to exclude native blacks, Mexicans, and other persons of color from the educational opportunities and resources afforded to whites. The Texas superintendent who bowed to local interests in denying Mexican American children access to schooling admitted this roughly two decades after Texas passed its compulsory attendance law in 1915.

As a result, during the Industrial Era, school systems in the Northeast were the most developed, best resourced, and most capable of enforcing universal compliance with compulsory attendance; thus, they were the school systems most capable of providing relatively equal access to expanding educational opportunities. Midwestern and western states followed closely behind the Northeast. Conversely, in the Industrial Era South, amid the institutionalized segregation and racial exclusion of Jim Crow, school systems were less mature and developed, had relatively fewer resources, and exercised less institutional control over children's schooling and work activities.

The unevenness in the expansion of educational opportunities for Industrial Era American children is depicted in figures 5.1 and 5.2. Figure 5.1 shows the average amount spent in each U.S. region on instruction per student enrolled in the state public school system from 1918 to 1958. (Recall from chapter 2 that this is the time span of the Biennial Survey of Education data.) The amounts are adjusted to 1940 dollar values so that real costs can be compared over time. Figure 5.2 presents the analogous trends for the average length of the public school term. Both are indicators of the degree of commitment to and investment in the provision of educational opportunities for children in a given school system.

In both figures, we see enormous gaps between the South and the other regions prior to World War II. With respect to expenditures, the southern disadvantage remained sizable up through 1958. The South did catch up to the other regions in the length of the school year when school systems nationwide converged to a standard 180-day academic year. However, this

Figure 5.1 *Educational Expenditures per Pupil (1940 Dollars), by U.S. Region, 1918–1958*

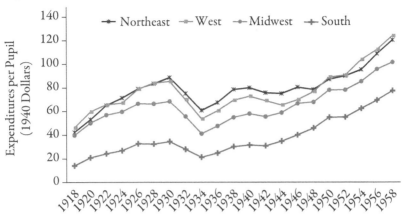

Source: Biennial Survey of Education, 1918–1958.

Figure 5.2 *Average Length of the Public School Term (Days), by U.S. Region, 1918–1958*

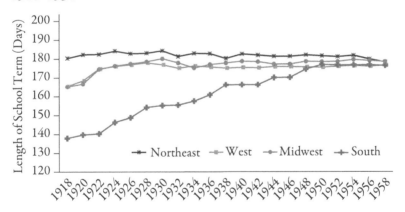

Source: Biennial Survey of Education 1918–1958.

convergence did not occur until the 1950s. For most of the first half of the twentieth century, children growing up in the South faced huge disadvantages relative to children in other regions in the sheer amount of schooling opportunities and instruction provided over the course of the year. The average child in the South entering the first grade in 1920 received about 43 fewer days of classroom instruction than a first-grade peer in the Northeast in their first year of schooling. This deficit accumulated to 167 days by the fourth grade. In other words, by the fourth grade, the average child in the Northeast had received nearly a full academic year's worth of instruction more than a child in the South. By the eighth grade, the deficit had increased to 306 days—nearly two academic years of instruction.

If all immigrant ethnoracial groups had been randomly distributed across the country during the Industrial Era, regional variation in school investment would play no role in explaining group differences in educational attainment. However, this was not the case. During the first half of the twentieth century, different ethnoracial groups, such as Italians, Mexicans, and native blacks, were exposed to very different institutional contexts. As we saw in chapter 4, the overwhelming majority of European immigrants and their offspring were heavily concentrated in growing industrial urban centers in the Northeast and Midwest, where relatively mature and well-funded school bureaucracies had long been in place.

Conversely, Industrial Era Mexicans' contexts of schooling were more heterogeneous. The two states with the largest concentrations of Mexican-origin children, California and Texas, adopted vastly different approaches to the schooling and integration of the children of immigrants. For example, in 1930 California spent 2.4 times as much on instruction per pupil as Texas. There were even large variations in school funding within Texas. In 1930, Bexar County, home of San Antonio, spent more on school instruction per pupil than other cities in Texas: 75 percent more than Hidalgo County, home of McAllen, and 50 percent more than Nueces County, home of Corpus Christi.[7]

It is important to note that these figures reflect funding and schooling opportunities distributed across *all* children and thus mask the variation in funding across ethnoracial groups. In the early twentieth century in both Texas and California, Mexican American children typically attended segregated Mexican schools. As discussed in chapter 4, public school funding tended to be diverted to white schools, leaving the Mexican schools within the same district with even less funding.

School Contexts and Mexican American Educational Mobility

What difference would it have made if Mexican American children had been given the opportunity to attend well-funded schools? A lot. Our data show that such an opportunity would have diminished and might even have erased some of the disadvantages typically accruing to Mexican American children on account of their ethnoracial or class background.

We specifically examined how school funding at age five was related to adult educational attainment among early-vintage, second-generation Mexican Americans and native whites. We relied on the BSE data (described in chapter 2) to measure variation in school expenditures per pupil at the county level. We appended these measures to the individual records of the second-generation Mexican American and native white children in the early vintage. We then examined their educational attainment in adulthood. We focused on the size of the educational gap between native whites and Mexicans for people who grew up in a variety of different situations: those who attended well-funded schools compared to those who attended schools not as well funded, and those whose parents had low levels of education versus those whose parents had high education levels. To isolate the effects of school funding, we adjusted the results to account for group differences in several demographic, family, and county- and state-level characteristics. Notably, we even adjusted the results for two indicators of structural racism: the black-white literacy gap among adults in 1940, which reflects racial differences in educational opportunity when these adults were growing up in the decades around the turn of the twentieth century, and the ratio of farm owners to workers in 1935, which reflects the dominant hierarchical structure of agricultural production on large industrial farms and ranches in southern Texas and California. The inclusion of these two measures helped us isolate the effects of school funding from other potential manifestations of structural racism.[8]

The results, shown in figure 5.3, clearly demonstrate the leveling effects of schools for early-vintage Mexican Americans. Additional school funding was associated with greater educational attainment for all groups, but the effect was rather weak for native whites and those with moderately educated parents. This can be seen in the upper panel of figure 5.3 for children whose parents had eight years of schooling (the average for native whites at the time). For this more privileged group, the relationship between school funding and adult attainment is quite flat, even for Mexican Americans. Because of their families' social and economic resources, these children would do fairly well even if they attended poorly resourced schools.

School funding was crucial, however, for the Mexican Americans with low levels of parental education who made up the vast majority of early-vintage Mexican Americans. As shown in the lower panel of figure 5.3, we found that school funding helped close the gap between white children and Mexican American children whose parents had only four years of schooling (the average for early-vintage Mexican American children). In low-funded school systems (such as in Texas), the ethnoracial gap was quite large— about one and a half years. This large gap may be related to the practices in many Texas school districts that diverted funding away from Mexican schools. Attending a poorly funded school district may have left Mexican American students an even smaller piece of an already small pie. However, in better-funded school systems (such as in California), the ethnoracial gap closed entirely.

Figure 5.3 *Educational Attainment among Early-Vintage Second-Generation Mexican Americans and Native White Children, by Parental Education and Public School Expenditures, 1920–1940 Birth Cohorts*

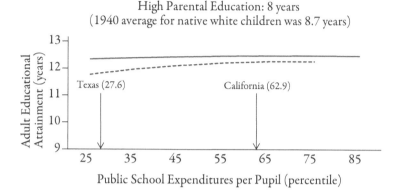

High Parental Education: 8 years
(1940 average for native white children was 8.7 years)

Public School Expenditures per Pupil (percentile)

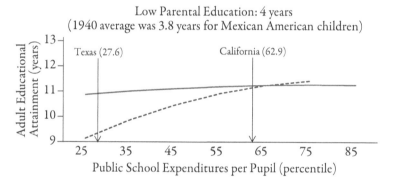

Low Parental Education: 4 years
(1940 average was 3.8 years for Mexican American children)

Public School Expenditures per Pupil (percentile)

—— Native white children   ---- Second generation Mexican Americans

Source: Analysis based on the IGENS-20 linked data files.

Notes: The sample includes second-generation Mexican and native white adults ages twenty-five and older in the early vintage (*N* = 707,000). Differences are adjusted for family structure, number of siblings, year of birth, gender, county characteristics (black-white differences in literacy, ratio of farm workers to owners, median home value, and urbanicity), and county fixed effects (see supplemental table 5.1). Any views expressed are those of the authors and not those of the U.S. Census Bureau. The Census Bureau has reviewed this data product to ensure appropriate access, use, and disclosure avoidance protection of the confidential source data used to produce it. This research was performed at a federal statistical research data center under FSRDC Project 2357 (CBDRB-FY23-0379).

Summary

In this chapter, we sought to better understand the contextual factors that might account for the differences in educational mobility observed in previous chapters between Industrial Era Europeans (chapter 3) and Mexican Americans (chapter 4). Our investigation focused on the role played by the nation's expanding public education system. This expansion was led by states whose school systems were relatively well developed and well resourced and where, during the Industrial Era, the Progressive and Americanization movements worked to promote the civic integration of immigrant ethnic groups through education. The children of poor and socially marginalized European immigrants grew up overwhelmingly in these advantageous school contexts.

The children of Industrial Era Mexican immigrants grew up primarily in one of two states, California or Texas. It would not be inaccurate to characterize Mexican American schooling experiences in these two states as so different that one could easily imagine they were located in two entirely different countries. Industrial Era California, heavily influenced by the Progressive movement, was home to one of the most developed and well-resourced school systems in the country. From historical education statistics, we can see that, like other Progressive education contexts, California spent more per capita on education overall than other states *and* devoted notable resources to Americanization and night school efforts. Conversely, the school systems in Jim Crow Era Texas were poorly funded and oriented toward achieving social outcomes that stood in direct philosophical contrast to integration through Americanization by upholding a system of racial segregation that overtly blocked or constrained minorities' opportunities for social mobility.

Failing to account for the different average schooling contexts faced by different groups could lead to misguided conclusions that differential patterns of educational mobility may be explained by the characteristics, motivations, and beliefs of the groups themselves. We conceive of school systems that promote the mission of Americanization, such as those in California, as *ethnocentric* institutional structures oriented around the goal of integrating civic society through the formal and universal education of "good Americans" from diverse ethnocultural backgrounds. Because the logic of this institutional arrangement is organized around the blurring of group boundaries, we expected that Mexican American mobility from the first to the second generation would resemble that of the European ethnic groups. Conversely, we conceive of schools in the Jim Crow South, including Texas, as structurally *racist* contexts of educational opportunity. Because such contexts produce bright and difficult boundaries and constraints on opportunity, we hypothesized that Mexican American mobility patterns anchored in Texas would lock in place a permanent gap in attainment, similar to the experience of native blacks.

We found strong support for these expectations in the data.

Indeed, we see strong evidence of the leveling effects of public school investment. In less-developed systems, we find large ethnoracial differences in school participation. In school contexts that are more developed and better funded, however, we find only small and insignificant differences in attainment across ethnoracial groups. These leveling effects were especially large among children whose parents had little schooling themselves. Thus, these contexts are crucial to immigrant integration insofar as they neutralize class disadvantages concentrated among second-generation immigrant children.

~ Chapter 6 ~

A Fair Shot

During his 2020 presidential campaign, Joe Biden frequently talked about the value of a level playing field for middle- and working-class people. At one campaign event, he emphasized the importance of just needing a fair shot:

> The very wealthy, they're a lot of good people, but they don't need my help. But families I came from need my help, and just need a shot, just a chance, just a chance to make it. When they've had that chance, they've never let the country down.[1]

The preceding chapters have illustrated the importance of a level playing field for the integration of immigrants during the Industrial Era, when equal access to schooling helped poor Italian and other SCE European immigrant families, break the cycle of poverty. For children of immigrants who had access to the same schools and the same public resources as native white children—as was the case for the children of Industrial Era European immigrants throughout the country and for the small number of children of Mexican immigrants who lived in the Midwest—school attendance rates and educational attainment levels were as high as those of the children of native whites, if not higher. However, when and where children were relegated to poorly funded schools and even deliberately discouraged from attending school—as were many Mexican American children in Texas—they lagged in school enrollment, average years of education, and attainment of a college degree. No doubt there were important variations and exceptions to these generalizations, but the broad-brush evidence we have uncovered thus far is clear: few early-vintage Mexican immigrants who moved to the United States during the early twentieth century had a "fair shot," and their

https://doi.org/10.7758/fhka5464.3968

disadvantage is evident to this day in the lives of their children and grand-children.

The contrast between Mexicans and Italians helps drive home our key point: integration hinges on a group's level of institutional inclusion. By institutional inclusion we mean equal treatment under the law and equal access to public resources. It is the opposite of structural racism. In the United States, many immigrant groups, including most European-origin immigrants, were institutionally included upon arrival either on account of their racial, ethnic, religious, and cultural similarity to U.S. citizens or because of legal precedent established by earlier battles for civil rights. The struggles that other immigrants have had to fight for their rights through some combination of social protests and court battles can take decades or longer. Italian immigrants arrived with nearly as little education as Mexican immigrants. Both groups experienced an unwelcoming social environment, and both were favored by employers for their work ethic. Still, Mexican Americans have had to engage in a much more prolonged fight for their civil rights than Italian Americans did. The barriers posed by racist institutional contexts, especially in Jim Crow Texas, led to Mexican Americans being denied equal access to good schools, middle-class jobs, and integrated neighborhoods. America's unequal Industrial Era playing field put Mexican Americans on dramatically different trajectories than Italian Americans.

In this chapter, we examine this claim further by focusing on a group that is relevant for contemporary American society: middle- and late-vintage Mexican Americans who came of age during the post–Civil Rights Era. Alongside native blacks, early-vintage Mexican Americans organized and fought in the civil rights movements of the 1950s and 1960s. These struggles are still ongoing, but their efforts appear to have at least partially paid off for the Mexican immigrants who came after them. As we show, these middle- and late-vintage Mexican Americans experienced significantly greater intergenerational educational mobility and attainment than early-vintage Mexican Americans.

This outcome is important for two reasons: First, it teaches a lesson about the importance of having a fair shot for the integration of immigrants and their descendants. Particularly for nonwhite groups like Mexican Americans whose rights easily could erode in the future given the direction of contemporary U.S. politics, it is important to remain vigilant if the country is to reach equity in educational outcomes in the future. Second, despite the concerns just noted, our analysis paints a cautiously optimistic picture for future generations of Mexican Americans. More than their early-vintage counterparts, later-vintage, second-generation Mexican immigrants grew up in circumstances that are similar to those we might expect and hope to see in the future, and their improved outcomes can be more plausibly interpreted as a harbinger for future generations of Mexican Americans.

Mexican Americans' Struggle for Civil Rights

Mexican Americans' struggle for greater access to schooling started with a fight for civil rights and institutional inclusion, a movement that ran parallel to and was reinforced by the African American social movements of the mid-twentieth century. Despite the ending of slavery and establishment of birthright citizenship with the passage of the Thirteenth and Fourteenth Amendments to the U.S. Constitution, there were substantial setbacks in the struggle for equality during the late 1800s and early 1900s, owing to the passage of laws, intimidation, and vigilante violence that aimed to segregate and disenfranchise African Americans and other nonwhite groups, including Mexican Americans in Texas. Significant progress was not made until after World War II.

The war shook up the racial social order when African Americans and Hispanics were called to serve in the military and work in skilled jobs vacated by white men. The Fair Employment Practices Committee (FEPC), created by executive order in 1941 to increase production in the government and defense sectors, was "charged with the task of seeing that no federal agency or company doing business with the government discriminated against any person because of race, color, creed, or national origin."[2] After FEPC field operations were begun in the Southwest in 1943, Mexican workers started being employed in skilled jobs at industrial plants. In 1946, employment offices for government jobs were turned back to state control, and there was an attempt to revert back to the prewar discriminatory practices. Montejano notes that Mexicans who were registered for skilled jobs were never referred to the employers calling for such skills and instead were referred to common labor jobs.[3] By then, though, it was too late. According to contemporary observer Pauline Kibbe in her book *Latin Americans in Texas*, "A new consciousness was evident." Latin Americans had "become more vocal in protesting the restrictions and inequalities with which they are confronted."[4]

At the same time, structural changes made it difficult for southern growers to control labor as they had during the Jim Crow Era. Rapid urbanization and the expansion of the manufacturing sector increased opportunities for rural sharecroppers and laborers, making it possible for them to walk away from poorly paying jobs and inhumane working conditions.[5] World War II had accelerated urbanization and industrialization, and growth in corporate farming and the mechanization of farm labor further reduced the need for manual labor and eroded the political power of small farmers. U.S. government officials and politicians also felt international pressure to improve conditions for nonwhites if they were to lead the world in condemning fascism and communism.[6]

These changes set the stage for collective action. As is well known, African Americans organized mass protests, marches, sit-ins, Freedom Rides, and strikes, often at risk to their lives, to challenge residential and school segregation, housing and employment discrimination, and restrictions on voting. Eventually a series of landmark Supreme Court rulings and civil rights legislation expanded the institutional inclusion of racial and ethnic minorities. The 1954 *Brown v. Board of Education* Supreme Court decision banned de jure school segregation by race (although de facto segregation continues).[7] The 1964 Civil Rights Act ended segregation in public places and banned employment discrimination on the basis of race, color, religion, sex, or national origin.[8] The 1965 Voting Rights Act banned racial discrimination in voting, leading to dramatic increases in voter turnout.[9] In Mississippi alone, voter turnout among African Americans increased from 6 percent in 1964 to 59 percent in 1969.[10] The 1968 Fair Housing Act banned discrimination based on race in rental and housing markets.[11] Although interpersonal and structural racism persist, both Hispanics and blacks are now treated as protected groups under these laws.

Despite their similarities, the social struggles of Hispanics and African Americans have not been the same. Hispanics' goals and strategies often diverged from those of African Americans. For one, Mexican Americans (and most Hispanics) have held a highly variable and ambiguous position as both white and nonwhite.[12] Mexican Americans were legally defined as white (and therefore eligible for U.S. citizenship) by the Treaty of Guadalupe Hidalgo, which brought an end to the 1846–1848 Mexican-American War. But they were not treated as white in all places or at all times. Early in the twentieth century in Texas, Tejano organizations used their "white" legal status to claim a higher standing in Texas communities, effectively distancing themselves from both African Americans and newly arriving Mexican immigrant laborers.[13] Claims of "whiteness" later created problems for them in courts when segregationists argued that Mexican Americans did not need to be represented on juries because whites were already represented and Mexican Americans were legally white. This argument became moot in 1954 when the Supreme Court ruled in *Hernandez v. Texas* that the Fourteenth Amendment applied to all racial and ethnic groups facing discrimination, effectively broadening civil rights laws to include Hispanics and all other nonwhites.[14]

Another distinction between African American and Hispanic social movements is that Hispanic social movements have frequently focused on issues related to immigrants and their children, such as labor conditions for migrant farm workers, the provision of bilingual education to non-English-speaking children, and undocumented children's access to public schooling and in-state tuition at public colleges and universities.[15] These issues continue to be debated in legislatures and litigated in courts, where they are often tied to civil rights law. For example, efforts to prevent the Trump administration from enacting its public charge rules, which sought to penalize noncitizens for using public benefits, were based on arguments that these rules would have a disparately harmful impact on Hispanics and other nonwhites.[16]

School Segregation

Equal access to good schools was a major focus of Mexican Americans' fight for equality, and in the 1930s much of the focus was on the common practice of segregating Mexican American children into underfunded schools. Mexican American children were segregated in both Texas and California, even though they were legally defined as "white."[17] School administrators argued that segregation was necessary because Mexican American children were too poor, too dirty, or not intelligent enough to attend Anglo schools. Teachers and administrators were documented as having negative views of Mexican Americans as dirty, lazy, uninterested in education, and better suited for manual labor. Segregationists backed their assertions with studies showing that Mexican Americans had lower IQ scores than Anglos.[18] Of course, we know now that IQ scores are strongly correlated with family income, English language proficiency, and prior schooling, and that they are not indicative of any inherent intellectual ability. Another common justification was that Mexican American children needed to be segregated from Anglo children until they learned English. This argument too was disingenuous, as integration almost never occurred, even after Mexican American children learned English.

Court decisions from the 1930s and 1940s, including the *Salvatierra* (1930), *Mendez* (1946), and *Delgado* (1948) decisions, outlawed school segregation for Mexican American children. For example, in the 1946 *Mendez* case, brought against the Westminster School District of Orange County, California, the Ninth Circuit Court of Appeals ruled that it was unconstitutional and unlawful to forcibly segregate Mexican American students by focusing on Mexican ancestry, skin color, and the Spanish language.[19]

Nevertheless, these court rulings did little to reduce segregation. In Texas, state authorities did nothing other than stop designating schools as "Mexican" in their official correspondence and publications. Opposition to the 1954 *Brown v. Board of Education* decision was vehement. Preachers, retired generals, and politicians all railed against the evils of desegregation.[20] In defiance, three statewide referenda that preserved school segregation, strengthened laws against interracial marriage, and supported local rule over federal intrusion passed in Texas in 1956 by four-to-one margins.

The tide started to turn as Mexican Americans gained political power. In 1965, the U.S. Supreme Court ruled that representatives must be distributed in proportion to population, which had the effect of rebalancing political power from rural to urban areas in Texas.[21] By 1967, there were fewer representatives in the Texas State Legislature who supported rural prejudices. By 1969, the Texas House rescinded the segregationist laws that had been passed in 1956.

Despite changes in segregation law, de facto school segregation continued. For example, desegregation efforts in California became challenging as new waves of immigrants continued to arrive and schools were expected to meet the needs of English Language Learners (ELL). The provision of bilingual education was in tension with efforts to desegregate schools. In his study of the Brownfield School System in California, Rubén Donato writes that desegregation efforts were difficult to carry out in part because of inherent clashes between desegregation mandates and the institutional requirements to run effective bilingual programs, which tended to cluster children into schools and classrooms according to their language needs.[22] School districts also found ways to technically meet the desegregation mandates while actually changing very little, such as delineating new boundaries and altering the very definition of segregation.

To this day, de facto segregation continues for Mexican American children. To demonstrate this point, we assembled data on the racial-ethnic composition of schools from 1987 (the earliest year available) to 2015.[23] We calculated a measure of segregation called the "dissimilarity index" for Hispanic students at both the district and school levels. The National Center for Education Statistics (NCES), the government agency that produces these statistics, reports enrollment information only under the category of Hispanic rather than specifically for Mexican Americans.

The dissimilarity index ranges from 0 to 100, with 100 indicating the highest level of segregation. At the district level, the index tells us the percentage of Hispanic children who would have to change districts to match the distribution of non-Hispanic White children within the state. The index is sensitive to regional patterns of Hispanic and non-Hispanic white settlement, but it may also reflect efforts to uphold segregation by strategically drawing district boundaries between "Hispanic" and "white" areas of a city. At the school level, the dissimilarity index indicates the percentage of Hispanic children who would have to change schools to match the distribution of non-Hispanic White children within their districts. The school-level measure reflects residential segregation within the district and the degree to which the district promotes integration through measures such as magnet schools and busing.

Results for the top two settlement states for Mexican immigrants, California and Texas, are shown in figure 6.1. District-level segregation declined by six points in Texas (from fifty-eight to fifty-two) and by two points in California (from fifty to forty-eight). At the school level, however, segregation increased between 1987 and the mid-2010s (from thirty-six to forty in California and from thirty-three to thirty-five in Texas), before declining a bit. Overall, there was little change in school- or district-level segregation over the last few decades.

Figure 6.1 *School Segregation (Dissimilarity Index) between Hispanic Children and Non-Hispanic White Children, 1987–2015*

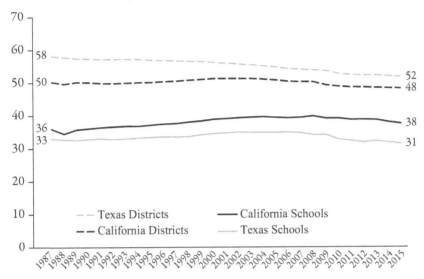

Source: Estimates based on 1987–2015 Common Core of Data (CCD) collected by the U.S. Department of Education.

Notes: The CCD is the primary database on public elementary and secondary education in the United States, and it includes data from all public schools. Segregation between Hispanic and non-Hispanic white students is measured using the dissimilarity index, which is the share of students who would have to change schools within a district (school-level segregation) or change districts within the state (district-level segregation) in order to achieve an even distribution.

We suspect that delayed progress in school integration may be related to both residential segregation and the organizational constraints facing schools. Because the Hispanic population has been continually replenished by new immigrants, residential segregation among Hispanics has not changed much since 1990.[24] Immigration from Mexico increased substantially during the 1990s and early 2000s, with the majority of new arrivals undocumented.[25] Mexican immigrants, especially the undocumented, tend to live with family and friends in coethnic neighborhoods.[26] Residential segregation may also persist because later-generation Mexican Americans experience "delayed spatial assimilation," meaning that they are slow to move into middle-class suburban neighborhoods.[27] Sociologist Jody Vallejo argues that second-generation, middle-class Mexican Americans are less likely to move to higher-income neighborhoods than other middle-class groups because their kinship networks are composed disproportionately of poor, undocumented immigrants.[28] They have both social and financial obligations to support their relatives and may be unable to move away or save money for a new home. Third, schools have struggled to meet the language-learning needs of immigrant students, leading school districts to concentrate bilingual programs in selected schools for organizational efficiency.[29]

Increasing and Equalizing School Funding

Another persistent focus for Mexican American reform movements has been to improve the quality of schooling. Regardless of ethnoracial background, the quality of schooling improved and became more uniform across and within states during the post–World War II Era as the nation sought to modernize its public school system.

The rising commitment to public schooling can be seen by examining state trends in public school expenditures, shown in figure 6.2. We obtained these estimates by compiling reports available from the NCES. We expressed all figures in 1940 dollars. Even after making this adjustment for inflation, school funding increased so much over the last century that we could not represent the raw data in a meaningful way on the same chart. A difference of $10 in funding was meaningful in 1920, given that the average expenditure per student was only $38, but $10 was a drop in the bucket in 2020, when funding was $733 per student (in 1940 dollars). To adjust, we plotted school funding figures on a logarithmic scale. With this transformation, each successive horizontal gridline represents twice the funding level of the previous gridline. In other words, the chart plots *relative* differences—such as one state providing double the funding provided by another state—as the same distance regardless of whether the *absolute* funding level is low (as it was in the beginning of the twentieth century) or high (as in the latter half of the twentieth century).

Remarkably, school funding increased twentyfold across the last century, even for figures that account for inflation. Additionally, inequality in funding across states narrowed over time. During the pre–Civil Rights Era (before 1950), the two states where most Mexican Americans lived—California and Texas—differed dramatically in public school spending. In 1930, California spent two and a half times as much as Texas did on its students. However, these differences narrowed during the Civil Rights Era, a time period that spanned the 1950s and 1960s. In 1950, California spent just 20 percent more per student than Texas. By the second decade of the post–Civil Rights Era (a period we define as starting in 1970), Texas caught up to California and even exceeded California's funding levels between 1988 and 2004. Today school funding levels continue to rise in many states, including California, although funding levels in Texas have stagnated and since 2016 have fallen behind California by more than 10 percent.

Figure 6.2 *Total Expenditures per Pupil by State (1940 Dollars), 1918–2020*

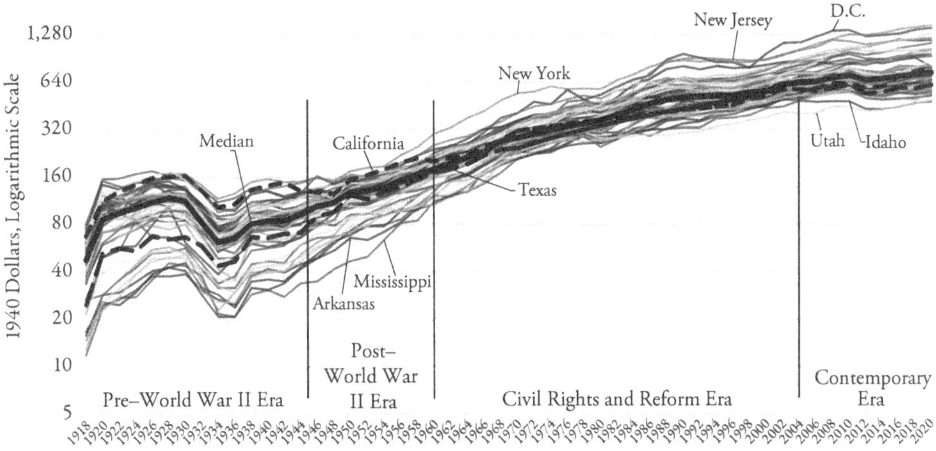

Sources: Biennial Survey of Education, 1918–1958; U.S. Department of Education, 1960–1986; Common Core of Data 1987–2020.

The rise in school funding was part of a broader movement to increase the quality and consistency of public education throughout the United States during the postwar years and the Civil Rights Era. Besides increasing funding, efforts were made to consolidate smaller into larger school districts and to grant greater authority to centralized educational agencies to impose educational standards on all public schools in a state. California school districts were instructed to develop consolidation plans to save on administrative costs and to expand curricular offerings.[30] Middle-class parents largely supported these efforts because consolidation carried benefits for their children (for example, better sports programs and programs for children with special needs). These changes ultimately led to better educational opportunities for Mexican American children because of their greater access to better schools, more uniform curricular offerings, and state-imposed regulations for school attendance and the duration of the school year.

Still, the resources allocated to schools attended by Mexican American students continued to lag. We compared the average expenditures per pupil in school districts attended by at least 30 percent Mexican American students and no more than 20 percent non-Hispanic, nonwhites ("Mexican districts") with expenditures per pupil in districts attended by at least 80 percent non-Hispanic white students and no more than 20 percent non-Hispanic, nonwhites ("white districts"). We can compile this data for as early as 1940, but only for districts in urban areas with at least ten thousand people. For 1952 and later, we have data for most non-rural districts.

In 1940, the average urban Mexican district spent 21 percent less than white districts in Texas and 35 percent less in California. By 1952, during the postwar period when spending on public schools increased rapidly across the country, Mexican districts still spent less. This was the case for urban Mexican districts and all Mexican districts in both Texas and California. In Texas, the gap in expenditures between Mexican and white districts was about the same as in 1940. In California, the funding gap closed somewhat between 1940 and 1952 but remained substantial. Mexican urban districts spent about 23 percent less than white districts, and all Mexican districts spent 10 percent less. These figures probably underestimate the inequality in funding because they reflect averages across all the schools in a district. Historians have documented many cases in which schools attended mostly by Mexican students were underfunded while neighboring white schools received a disproportionate share of school funds.

During the 1950s and 1960s in Los Angeles, Mexican American students did not have access to the same educational opportunities as Anglo students. Over half (60 percent) dropped out before finishing high school, and the average reading level of those who did graduate was that of an eighth-grade Anglo student.[31] Schools funneled many Mexican American students into vocational programs and discouraged them from going to college. In response, students began to organize. In March 1968, about fifteen thousand students walked out of their classrooms in protest in an event that came to be known as the "East Los Angeles Walkouts." With the help of their newly formed Educational Issues Coordinating Committee (EICC), they presented a list of demands to the Los Angeles Board of Education, including recommendations for curriculum changes, bilingual education, and the hiring of Mexican American administrators. Although their demands were not met at the time, they helped unify and embolden the Chicano movement to demand better educational opportunities.

In the same year, 1968, in San Antonio, Texas, Demitrio Rodriguez and a group of like-minded San Antonio parents filed a class action lawsuit on behalf of minority students from low-income school districts.[32] Rodriguez was the son of a migrant farmworker who grew up in the 1950s in Texas and had to quit school after the sixth grade. He wondered why the conditions in his children's school in the Edgewood School District—leaky windows, a lack of air conditioning, and a condemned third floor—were so much worse than in the neighboring nearly all-white Alamo Heights School District. Rodriguez's chief complaint was that the Edgewood School District, whose student body was predominantly Mexican American, received only $37 per pupil while funding for students in Alamo Heights was $413 per pupil.[33] "He wasn't just thinking about me and my brothers at that time. He was thinking about the kids and the future kids that were coming," said his son, Alex Rodriguez, in a 2015 interview.[34]

Rodriguez's efforts spanned several decades. The Supreme Court ruled in 1973 that there was no constitutional right to an equal education (*San Antonio ISD v. Rodriguez*), and that the problem needed to be addressed at the state level.[35] However, Rodriguez, the Mexican American Legal Defense and Educational Fund (MALDEF), and parent associations challenged Texas's school funding system again in the 1980s. By now, Rodriguez was advocating on behalf of his grandchildren, and this time the outcome was different. The Texas Supreme Court reversed its earlier ruling and held in *Edgewood Independent School District v. Kirby* that Texas's school financing system was unconstitutional.[36] This was just one example of immigrants from an earlier vintage working to expand opportunities for later vintages. His lawyer, Albert Kauffman, recalled that Rodriguez "came from an environment in the '50s and '60s where Mexican Americans were treated so badly and poor people were treated so badly and I think he early on decided to focus his energies for the rest of his life on doing something about that."[37]

These efforts ultimately paid off for Mexican Americans living in Texas. In an effort led by Ross Perot, the Texas State Legislature passed a law in 1984 to equalize funding across school districts in Texas by capping property tax rates for schools and distributing revenues from wealthier to poorer districts. The new law also reduced class sizes, toughened academic standards, mandated testing for teachers, linked teachers' raises to performance, and required students to pass all their courses or else give up extracurricular activities like team sports.[38] Students' test scores climbed steadily, and the dropout rate fell from 34 percent to 21 percent by 1990, six years after the passage of the law. Critics argued that the reforms focused too much on rulemaking and too little on setting goals for students and letting teachers help them achieve those goals. In addition, huge inequities remained between rich and poor school districts, leading to further court challenges. Nevertheless, the reforms sent a clear signal that the status quo was no longer acceptable. According to Frank Newman, president of the Education Commission of the States, the reforms said: "Attention! The old world of half-baked schools isn't good enough."[39]

School funding within Texas is now much less unequal than it was in the 1940s and 1950s (see figure 6.3). In 1990, Mexican districts spent on average 3 percent *more* per pupil than the average white district. On the other hand, in California, where Mexican districts spent 9 percent less than white districts, the situation was not appreciably different from what it had been in 1952. Another telling statistic derives from a comparison of the actual dollars going to Mexican districts in Texas with California. In 1990, the figures were nearly identical in the two states: about $3,700 per pupil in 1990 dollars. By 2000, spending for Mexican districts in Texas exceeded California by 9 percent, and by 2010, Texas exceeded California by 21 percent.

Figure 6.3 *Funding Differences between "Mexican" and "White" Districts, Texas and California, 1940–2010*

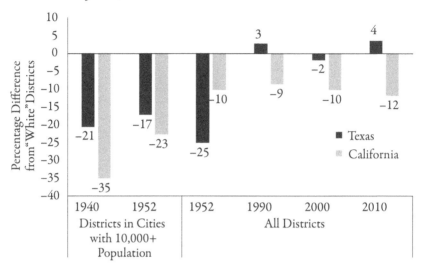

Sources: Biennial Survey of Education, 1918–1958; Common Core of Data, 1990, 2000, and 2010.

Notes: "White districts" = at least 80 percent white and less than 20 percent non-Hispanic, nonwhite students. "Mexican districts" = at least 30 percent Mexican and less than 20 percent non-Hispanic, nonwhite students. Negative numbers indicate that Mexican districts on average receive less funding than white districts, and positive numbers indicate the opposite. Funding differences are expressed as a percentage of "white" district funding levels: (Mexican – white)/white × 100.

Educational Equity

Although it is important to equalize resources across public schools, equal funding may not be enough to reduce inequality in children's outcomes. Some children come from homes characterized by low English proficiency, poverty, and low parental education. Educating these children may require more special services and more time and attention from teachers. This insight led to the next stage in educational reform in the United States: a switch from a focus on equality in inputs to an equity-based framework that seeks to equalize outcomes. An equity-based framework recognizes that school districts must provide something different to non-English-speaking and immigrant children to bring them up to speed with other students.

Equity principles were prominent in the push for bilingual education. Concerned that their children could not understand their teachers, Mexican American parents advocated for bilingual education. For example, Donato describes how Mexican Americans attended school board meetings and confronted school board members, arguing that the current "bilingual efforts [were] not enough," and that "until bilingual education is given support, it will continue to be an unwanted stepchild."[40] During this time period, 76 percent of Mexican American children ages five to eighteen lived in Spanish-speaking households and stood to benefit from bilingual classes.

In 1968, President Lyndon Johnson signed the Bilingual Education Act, which recognized the educational needs of students with limited English proficiency and provided federal funds to schools to establish bilingual programs. A few years later, a group of Mexican American families filed a class action lawsuit against the Portales School District in New Mexico, a school system where the majority of students were Mexican American. The lawsuit claimed that the district engaged in discriminatory practices that denied equal educational opportunities to Spanish-surnamed students. In 1972, the U.S. Court for the District of New Mexico ruled in their favor and instructed the Portales School District to recruit bilingual teachers and adopt a curriculum that featured daily bilingual instruction to all Portales School District students (*Serna v. Portales*, 1974).[41] This decision was later upheld by the U.S. Supreme Court's 1974 *Lau v. Nichols* decision, which ruled in favor of non-English-speaking Chinese students in San Francisco, holding that by not receiving instruction in a language they could understand, they had been deprived of an education in violation of the 1964 Civil Rights Act.[42]

Equity principles also were embodied in the school reforms in the 1990s and 2000s that held schools responsible for meeting learning standards for all children, including children who might seem harder to reach, such as those from poor families and those with limited English proficiency. In the early 1990s, Governor George W. Bush built upon prior initiatives started in Texas by Ross Perot and Governor Ann Richards to improve children's school performance. Borrowing from a business model, he held educators accountable for their students' performance on the Texas Assessment of Academic Skills (TAAS) test. Under the reforms passed in 1993, Texas schoolchildren were not allowed to graduate or advance to the next grade if they failed the TAAS tests on reading, writing, and math, although they were given opportunities to retake the tests if they failed. Additionally, administrators' job prospects—and bonuses that could total thousands of dollars—depended on their students' school attendance, dropout rates, and TAAS scores.

A crucial element of the plan was the requirement that schools report on these metrics separately for racial/ethnic minority groups and economically disadvantaged students, thus shining a light on inequality in children's learning. Rewards for educators were tied to equity in achievement across all groups. Dubbed the "Texas Miracle" by some, test scores improved dramatically, particularly for minority children. For example, the share of Hispanic children passing all sections of the eighth-grade TAAS tests more than doubled, from 32 percent in 1994 to 67 percent in 1999.[43] The apparent success of the plan helped propel Bush to the White House, where he re-packaged his plan as the No Child Left Behind Act (NCLB). NCLB was passed by the U.S. Congress in 2002 and then reauthorized and revised in 2015 by President Barack Obama as the Every Student Succeeds Act.[44] Similar to the Texas plan, NCLB required schools to report on and be held accountable for all students' learning, regardless of socioeconomic back-ground, ethnoracial identity, and English language proficiency. Until then, many states and school districts had been routinely exempting English Lan-guage Learners from mandated standardized testing.[45]

Many people criticized President Bush's approach to education. They argued that high-stakes testing led schools to emphasize test-taking skills on narrowly defined topics, taking the joy out of student learning and ex-ploration. Margaret Immel, a Rice University reading expert, remarked, "In many classrooms, the joy and magic of reading is being replaced with drudgery."[46] Others argued that the Texas Miracle was a mirage, because schools would find ways to increase test scores without enhancing student learning, such as by encouraging poor-performing students to drop out of high school. Some school administrators even faced charges of fraud for tampering with test results.

Nevertheless, holding schools accountable appeared to significantly boost test scores among Hispanic and limited-English-proficiency students, even on non-high-stakes tests like the National Assessment of Educational Progress (NAEP). Increases in NAEP test scores cannot be attributed to "cheating" by schools or efforts to teach to the test because NAEP tests are not used to hold schools accountable under NCLB. Using NAEP data, a team of economists at the Brookings Institute found that NCLB closed the white-Hispanic achievement gap in mathematics by 19 percent.[47] Others corroborated these findings and showed that NCLB's threat of sanctions was positively correlated with NAEP test score gains by low-performing students in "failing" schools, and that this improvement did not come at the expense of high-performing students in the same schools.[48]

Standardized testing has since become an important tool for advancing educational equity and inclusion. As argued by Melissa Lazarin, a senior policy analyst at the Migration Policy Institute:

> It comes as no surprise that many civil-rights groups, including the na-tion's largest Latino civil-rights organization, have deep reservations about reducing federal testing requirements. While states must continue to take steps to improve the quality and validity of their tests, watering down tests or dismissing them altogether may contribute to overlooking ELL [English Language Learners] and other students and misdirecting resources and support services away from where they are most needed.[49]

Improvement in Educational Attainment

The Civil Rights Era brought about dramatic improvements in Mexican Americans' access to education and in the quality of that education. The gains made were not simply provided by newly enlightened government officials and educators but were the result of decades of protest by Mexican American people.

We have already demonstrated that early-vintage Mexican Americans—those born to Industrial Era immigrants between 1920 and 1940—suffered great disadvantages in education, particularly those who lived in Texas. The improvements in public schooling appear to have increased Mexican Americans' educational mobility and leveled out regional variations in opportunity.

We compared educational outcomes across three groups of Mexican Americans who were children during different periods of the twentieth century—namely, those belonging to early-, middle-, and late-arriving vintages. Early-vintage Mexican American families arrived during the early twentieth century. Their second-generation children were born between 1920 and 1940, and many of their third-generation grandchildren are adults today. Middle-vintage families arrived during the middle of the twentieth century, and their U.S.-born children were born between 1960 and 1980. Finally, late-vintage families arrived mostly after 1965, and their U.S.-born children were born between 1980 and 1994. We do not yet have data for the grandchildren of the middle- and late-vintage immigrants because too few have reached adulthood. Nevertheless, we can compare the mobility experiences for the second generation across all three vintages.

We plotted the average years of schooling for each vintage by generation in figure 6.4. Each point on the chart represents the gap between Mexican Americans and their native white contemporaries, so points below the horizontal line indicate disadvantages for Mexican Americans.[50]

For early-vintage Mexican Americans, educational attainment relative to native whites increased slowly across generations. A substantial gap remained (nearly two years) by the third generation. The story is different for middle- and late-vintage Mexican Americans. First, middle- and late-vintage Mexican immigrants arrived in the United States in a slightly worse socioeconomic position than early-vintage Mexican Americans, though not because educational attainment had declined in Mexico; in fact, it had actually increased across the twentieth century. Rather, educational attainment in the United States increased even faster, so the gaps were larger for middle- and late-vintage immigrants.

A second important difference from early-vintage Mexican Americans is that second-generation Mexican Americans from the middle and late vintages experienced faster upward mobility. By the second generation, they

Figure 6.4 *Average Educational Attainment (Years) among Mexican-Origin Adults Ages Twenty-Five and Older Relative to Native Whites, by Generation and Vintage*

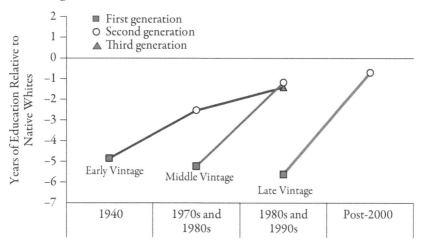

Source: IGENS-20 linked data files.

Notes: All differences from native whites are statistically significant. The Census Bureau's disclosure review board and disclosure avoidance officers have reviewed this information product for unauthorized disclosure of confidential information and approved the disclosure avoidance practices applied to this release. This research was performed at a federal statistical research data center under FSRDC Project 2357 (CBDRB-FY22-P2357-R9408).

came closer to closing the gap with native whites than early-vintage Mexican Americans of both the second and third generations. This is evident at all levels of education, including high school completion, postsecondary attainment, and college completion.[51] They did not close the gap entirely, but neither did other successful groups from the Industrial Era, including children of early-vintage Italian immigrants. In fact, the relative attainments of late-vintage, second-generation Mexicans are very similar to those of early-vintage, second-generation Italians. Italians fell behind their native white contemporaries by 0.6 years of schooling, while late-vintage Mexicans fell behind by 0.7 years.

Furthermore, the large regional variations in schooling among early-vintage Mexican Americans leveled out for the later vintages.[52] Early-vintage, second-generation Mexican Americans had three fewer years of schooling than native whites if they lived in the South (that is, in Texas), but only 1.9 fewer years in the West and one fewer year in the Midwest and Northeast. Among late-vintage Mexican Americans, however, the schooling gap shrank to less than a year in all regions. Moreover, and reflecting the impacts of educational reforms in Texas, the gap in the South (0.7 years) was less than in the West (0.9 years), and about the same as in the Midwest and Northeast (0.6 years).

To help grasp the magnitude of the gains made by Mexican Americans, we asked and answered a hypothetical question. What would have happened if early-vintage Mexican Americans had experienced the same degree of upward mobility as late-vintage Mexican Americans? What if they had benefited from the educational reforms of the late twentieth century? The results are shown in figure 6.5.[53] As labeled in the chart, the thick solid line indicates the observed educational attainments for early-vintage Mexican Americans, and the dashed line depicts the counterfactual scenario in which they had late-vintage mobility rates. For comparison, we provide parallel figures for native whites as a thin solid line and a dotted line.

To interpret the findings, we find it helpful to first focus on the results for native whites. Under the counterfactual scenario, educational attainment for native whites would have been roughly the same as their actual

Figure 6.5 *Attainment of Early-Vintage Mexican Americans and Native Whites and Counterfactual Attainment If the Early Vintage Experienced Late-Vintage Intergenerational Mobility*

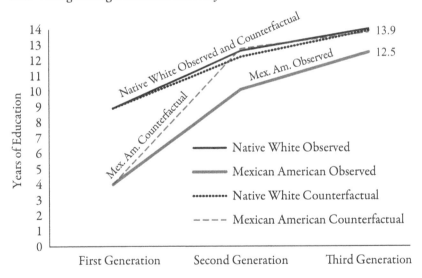

Source: IGENS-20 linked data files.

Notes: The Census Bureau's disclosure review board and disclosure avoidance officers have reviewed this information product for unauthorized disclosure of confidential information and approved the disclosure avoidance practices applied to this release. This research was performed at a federal statistical research data center under FSRDC Project 2357 (CBDRB-FY22-P2357-R9408).

outcome. We know this because the thin solid and dotted lines overlap. This suggests that native whites' mobility patterns did not change much between early and late vintages. In other words, the probability of attaining more (or less) education than one's parent did not change. However, the findings are different for Mexican Americans. Early-vintage Mexican Americans would have had much higher levels of education, and the gap between them and whites would have closed by the second generation if they had had the same educational mobility as late-vintage Mexican Americans. This is evident because the dashed line for second- and third-generation Mexican Americans overlaps with the black lines for native whites. Results were similar when we examined high school, postsecondary, and college attainment separately.[54] This indicates that educational mobility among Mexican Americans improved over time and eventually matched the mobility patterns seen among native whites.

Summary

In the decades following World War II, and especially during the 1990s and early 2000s, substantial improvements were made in the quality of the schools and instruction provided to Mexican American students. Although school segregation continues, school funding is higher and distributed more equitably than in the past. Additionally, equity-based policies appear to be improving learning outcomes for Hispanic and ELL students. These changes did not come about on their own or solely through the goodwill of individual educators. The heroes of this story are all the Mexican American people who protested, voted, and took their cases to court: the students who walked out of East Los Angeles schools; the parents who attended school board meetings to demand bilingual education; and the grandparents who, like Demitrio Rodriguez, fought in court for equitable school funding.

These efforts appear to have paid off. Large-scale structural changes in schooling were made because teachers, superintendents, and school boards were forced to make them. This included revising funding formulas to equalize funding across the schools in Texas and California. It also involved the passage of reforms and enactment of equity-based policies that required schools to do what was necessary for all children to succeed, even if that meant providing bilingual education and extra instruction to help the children of immigrants catch up with their schoolmates.

Because of these changes, middle- and late-vintage Mexicans have been much more successful in school than early-vintage Mexicans. Although they did not leapfrog over native whites, as some European-origin groups did, their educational trajectories look similar to those of early-vintage Italian Americans in that they were able to go far beyond their parents in school. In fact, early-vintage Mexican Americans would have closed the schooling gap with native whites if their upward mobility rates had been similar to those of middle- and late-vintage Mexican Americans. This suggests that if middle- and late-vintage Mexican Americans are to continue on their current path of upward mobility, they are likely to eventually be integrated with native whites.

~ Chapter 7 ~

Building New Walls

American's perpetual unease with immigration is captured in the lyrics of "Why We Build the Wall" in Anaïs Mitchell's musical *Hadestown*:

> Because they want what we have got
> The enemy is poverty
> And the wall keeps out the enemy.[1]

These lines sound like a critique of Donald Trump's promise to build a U.S.-Mexico border wall, but they really are a commentary on a much older characteristic of human societies: the fear of outsiders. Somewhat presciently, Mitchell wrote the lyrics in 2010, several years *before* Trump's 2016 presidential campaign. In a 2016 commentary, she said: "There is nothing new about the Wall. Political leaders have invoked it time and again to their advantage, because it works so well on people who feel scared."[2] Indeed, U.S. presidents of both political parties have made sustained efforts to build physical border walls over the last four decades. And in a metaphorical sense, the racist system of labor controls and segregation that took place in Texas during the first half of the twentieth century was a wall. That system significantly slowed down the integration of Mexican Americans by keeping them trapped in low-wage work and actively blocking their children's paths into the middle class.

In this final chapter, we look toward the future. As in the early twentieth century, the American nation is once again grappling with large-scale immigration. Currently, 27 percent of the population is an immigrant or a child of an immigrant, and of these, 28 percent are of Mexican descent. Still others are arriving from newer origins in Central America, South America, Asia, and Africa. Those from Central America especially are quite

https://doi.org/10.7758/fhka5464.3947

poor and have little education compared with the average American. Moreover, as the nation's population ages and fertility falls, demand for low-skilled immigrant labor in the agricultural, construction, and service sectors is likely to continue.[3] A recent Census Bureau analysis reported that the U.S. population would start to decline as early as 2024 if all immigration was halted.[4] Another report published by Jeffrey Passel and D'Vera Cohn indicates that *all* of the growth in the working-age population from 2015 to 2035 will come from immigrants who were not living in the United States in 2015.[5] In other words, the working-age population *will* shrink without immigration. Yet, as in the past, Americans are deeply divided about the value of large-scale immigration.

What will become of Mexican Americans living in the country today? Important progress has been made, but there has also been some backsliding. The MAGA movement has cultivated resentments among whites who fear being replaced by nonwhite immigrants, and its political leaders have falsely depicted immigrants (both legal and undocumented) as criminals and "snakes" seeking to bring drugs into the country and inflict harm on Americans.[6] Assuming that large-scale immigration continues, will the nation repeat its past mistake of building walls between "us" and "them," the next group of newcomers? Important lessons from the experiences of Mexican Americans across the twentieth century inform answers to this question and point to the conditions that create long-lasting disadvantages. In the remainder of the chapter, we describe these lessons and provide some conclusions about their application today.

Immigrant Starting Points

The first lesson of our study is that, under the right circumstances, immigrants' starting points are relatively unimportant. In the 1910s and 1920s, many Americans worried that the immigrants from Italy, and those from Southern, Central and Eastern (SCE) Europe, more broadly, would never become fully American. These immigrants seemed too poor and uneducated to be capable of success in this country. Such anxiety can undermine immigrant integration by leading employers and teachers to stereotype and discriminate against immigrants and their children. Fears that immigrants would never be successfully assimilated eventually led to the passage and enactment of the 1924 Johnson-Reed Act, which effectively shut down immigration from SCE Europe.

We know now that these concerns were shortsighted. As we showed in chapter 3, even the least-educated European immigrant group, the Italians, outperformed native whites in average educational attainment by the third generation. As Charles Hirschman has documented, immigrants and their children are overrepresented in science, film, music, and the arts.[7] The nation is more educated and culturally richer today than it would have been in the absence of immigration. Mired in the problems of their times, however, the early twentieth-century observers could not see the future clearly. They did not understand that immigrants' low starting points were much less important than whether they were treated fairly. They failed to see the potential of immigration as an engine of innovation and progress, and they could not imagine that the outsiders would soon become insiders.

We should feel reassured by this story and be careful not to underestimate new immigrants' potential for success. Yet once again we are anxious about immigrants, as aptly illustrated by Americans' concerns about the "quality" of the immigrants who are currently admitted to the United States. The term "quality" has been used by economist George Borjas for decades to refer to the education and skills with which immigrants arrive.[8] The word suggests that the characteristics that immigrants arrive with are embedded within them rather than a reflection of the opportunities they have had. The focus on starting points also leads people to ignore how most immigrants typically change as they spend time in the country.

Deeply influenced by Borjas and convinced that the "quality" of immigrants was declining, President Trump's team initiated a series of immigration policies to address the situation.[9] In addition to the Muslim ban, reductions in refugee admissions, and child separation policies, they proposed the RAISE (Reforming American Immigration for Strong Employment) Act. Much like the 1924 Johnson-Reed Act, the RAISE Act would have dramatically changed the number and types of immigrants admitted to the country. It would have reduced the number of family-based admissions and required all employment-based immigrants to enter either with a combination of very high levels of education, English language proficiency, and high earnings or with a record of extraordinary accomplishments or wealth.[10] Most legal immigrants currently admitted to the United States would not have qualified for admission under the RAISE Act.

The Trump team also worried that the United States—with its high standard of living and relatively generous social service programs—had become a "welfare magnet" to poor people in other countries. Accordingly, they sought to penalize immigrants who used public assistance—or seemed likely to use it in the future—by denying them admission, taking away their citizenship if they already had naturalized, and deporting them.[11] When asked by NPR's Rachel Martin whether he agreed with Emma Lazarus's words etched at the base of the Statue of Liberty, the Trump administration's acting director of U.S. Citizenship and Immigration Services, Ken Cuccinelli, indicated that he did, but added a line to the poem (in italics): "Give me your tired and your poor . . . *who can stand on their own two feet and who will not become a public charge.*"[12] In fact, these concerns are based on stereotypes rather than facts. Noncitizens are ineligible for most types of public assistance because of a welfare reform law passed in 1996 by President Bill Clinton.[13] Therefore, immigrants use welfare at lower rates than the U.S.-born.[14] Most assistance going to immigrant households is food assistance, and only the U.S.-born children living in their households are eligible for it.

Because of a series of court challenges and his 2020 election loss, Trump's proposals to change immigration policy were never enacted fully, but they still have had negative effects. For example, because of the threats to punish immigrants for using public programs, immigrants have been afraid to use governmental assistance even when it is legal and lifesaving to do so. Social scientists are just now finding evidence that, because they were less likely to seek financial assistance and health care during the COVID-19 pandemic, death rates among Hispanic immigrants were elevated.[15] One study conducted in California found that foreign-born Hispanics ages twenty to sixty-four were more than eleven times as likely to die from COVID as non-Hispanic whites, and more than three times as likely to die as U.S.-born Hispanics.[16]

Our overall message is that it is quite common to underestimate the contributions immigrants and their children are likely to make to the country, a mistake Americans have been making for hundreds of years. This response has led people to build physical and social walls between immigrants and themselves and to pressure lawmakers to propose and support punitive policies that attempt to restrict immigration to the "right" kind of people and limit immigrants' access to important public resources. The COVID-19 pandemic showed the tragic results of these policies, which, even in the best of times, can undermine the health of immigrants and their children and further delay their integration.

It is difficult to counter a fear and distrust of outsiders because these feelings seem to be immune to facts. Although we cannot offer simple solutions, it may be helpful to encourage Americans to explore their own family histories, learn about the support their ancestors once received when they were new to this country, and find commonalities with today's immigrants. Both of us (the authors) have integrated such discussions into our college courses on immigration. We ask our students to interview an immigrant or discuss their own family immigration story with a parent or grandparent. Such discussions, which often circle around the hardships and aspirations of both past and current immigrants, can help shrink the social distance between groups.

Structural Racism

A second lesson of our study is that structural racism has had long-lasting negative impacts that are transmitted from parents to their children and grandchildren. If you recall from chapter 4, structural racism goes beyond individual attitudes or racial slurs. It is embedded in systems, laws, and policies that determine which groups get access to power and resources. By digging into historical archives and old census records, we found that Mexican Americans' disadvantages today are deeply rooted in past systems of structural racism. Due to an exploitative system of labor controls, residential and school segregation, and underfunding of schools, immigrants' children did not have equal access to opportunities in Texas. Old interviews with superintendents and others in positions of authority reveal that this lack of access was not simply due to neglect or a lack of funds. It was deliberate.

We know just how harmful the situation was for Mexican Americans in Texas when we contrast their outcomes with outcomes for those in other parts of the country. Second-generation Mexican Americans obtained nearly as much schooling as Italian Americans and native whites if they moved to more progressive states like Illinois and California. Similar to the legacy of Jim Crow laws for African Americans, the disadvantages of early-vintage Mexican immigrants were passed on to their children and even their grandchildren. We calculated that immigrants' historical disadvantages explain between 60 and 80 percent of the educational disadvantages seen among third-generation Mexican Americans today.

We should be aware of this history when making judgments about the relative successes and failures of different immigrant groups. For example, it helps us clearly refute the assumptions underlying Tom Brokaw's suggestion in 2019 that Mexican Americans and other Hispanics should work harder to assimilate.[17] Mexican Americans' disadvantages stem from deliberate exclusion from educational opportunities more than from any lack of effort. This history also confirms that the pattern of third-generation delay among contemporary Mexican Americans is deeply rooted in past systems of structural racism, particularly in Texas, but should not necessarily be taken as a bellwether of integration for later-vintage Mexican Americans, a point on which we elaborate later in the chapter.

The costs of structural racism should serve as a warning about how not to treat immigrants in the future. Although opportunities for Mexican Americans have clearly improved since the early twentieth century, some areas of concern remain. One of the most significant structural barriers to integration for many immigrants living in the United States today is their lack of documentation and a viable path to legal immigration status. Unauthorized immigration often stems from a mismatch between labor demand and immigration law. Between 1942 and 1964, the Bracero Program permitted millions of Mexican farmworkers to live and work legally in the United States on temporary worker visas. However, the program was abruptly ended with the passage of the Immigration and Nationality Act of 1965. This change severely reduced the number of Mexicans who could migrate legally. Yet social and economic connections between Mexico and the American Southwest were already firmly established and demand for Mexican labor in the United States continued. The end of the Bracero Pro-

gram did not change this basic fact. As a consequence, the Mexican migration flow continued but was transformed from legal to unauthorized virtu-
ally overnight. Later, in the 1990s and early 2000s, the United States started
fortifying the U.S.-Mexico border to reduce unauthorized border crossings
despite robust labor demand. Rather than slowing new unauthorized migration, border enforcement disincentivized return migration.[18] It was risky
for unauthorized immigrants already living in the United States to leave the
country because they could not be certain that they would be allowed to
return to the United States. The consequence was that unauthorized Mexican immigrants became permanent residents, and the population grew dramatically.[19] According to the latest estimates produced by the Migration
Policy Institute, 5.2 million Mexican unauthorized immigrants were living
in the United States in 2021. In other words, *47 percent of the Mexican
foreign-born population* lacked legal status.[20]

Being an unauthorized immigrant severely reduces access to opportunities and resources. Like exploitative labor controls in early twentieth-
century Texas, unauthorized legal status raises a barrier between the immigrant and the opportunities available to others in the United States. For
example, it limits an individual's ability to work in jobs for which they
would otherwise be qualified. It bars them from receiving most public benefits, such as food assistance and non-emergency health care, and it can
limit their housing options.[21] Because of a Supreme Court ruling in 1982,
unauthorized immigrants must be provided with a public education up
through twelfth grade.[22] However, they still do not have access to in-state
tuition rates for public colleges and universities in twenty-six states.[23]

The negative impacts of unauthorized immigration status frequently
spill over to children. The most severe impact of immigration enforcement
is family separation.[24] Since about 2005, tougher interior immigration enforcement and a concomitant rise in deportations has dramatically increased the likelihood that the children of immigrants, especially those with
Latin American origins, will reside with just one parent or no parents at
all.[25] Parental deportation has more negative effects on children than other
kinds of separation (like divorce) because the deportation of a parent is associated with the loss of both the parent and the financial resources the parent would have contributed to the household. Parental separation and other
factors associated with having an undocumented parent negatively affect
children's emotional and behavioral development.[26]

The impact extends beyond deportation. Sociologist Joanna Dreby uses
the metaphor of a "deportation pyramid" to illustrate the far-reaching impacts of immigration enforcement on families.[27] Even though relatively
few children (at the top of the pyramid) experience the most severe consequences—the deportation of a parent and permanent family dissolu-
tion—many more children (at the base of the pyramid) experience other,
more diffused impacts, such as fear of family instability. Undocumented

legal status is also thought to impact parenting by restricting travel, limiting the extent to which parents access public programs and benefits on behalf of their children, and keeping them living in fear of the police (especially while driving).[28] By limiting the financial resources and opportunities of undocumented parents, these restrictions spill over to their U.S.-born children, a consequence of the immigration enforcement policies of the U.S. government that Laura Enriquez labels "intergenerational punishment."[29] Not surprisingly, one study estimated that the negative impacts of parental undocumented status significantly delay the assimilation and socioeconomic integration of Mexican Americans by at least a generation.[30]

One might wonder why so many come to the United States illegally if the cost of being an unauthorized immigrant is so high. A major reason is that the United States is addicted to unauthorized immigration. U.S. employers have come to depend on low-cost immigrant labor, and U.S. consumers benefit from low prices every time they purchase fresh fruits and vegetables or have their lawns cut, houses cleaned, and children supervised. Immigrants put up with this arrangement because they need the work.

Because of the demand for an exploitable labor force, there is little political will to enforce labor laws, particularly in sectors where immigrants work. For example, the United States has strong child labor laws, except in agriculture, a sector in which children as young as twelve or thirteen, many of them from immigrant families, may work. Indeed, we are just now seeing efforts in some states, like Arkansas in 2023, to further dilute child labor laws.[31] As *New York Times Magazine* writer Marcela Valdes argues:

> America's economy has always relied upon a mass of disempowered, foreign-born laborers, whether it was enslaved Africans picking cotton, Chinese building railroads, Irish digging coal, Italians sewing garments or Mexicans harvesting fruit. Even today, some sectors in the U.S. economy seem almost reserved for workers who have been deliberately kept vulnerable.[32]

When thinking about the future, it is good to know that unauthorized immigration from Mexico is in decline. Although the largest number of unauthorized immigrants continue to originate in Mexico, the size of the unauthorized Mexican immigrant population has declined 33 percent from the 7.7 million peak in 2007. The decline stems from changes in conditions in Mexico. Decreases in family size have reduced the pressures on people to work abroad to support their families, and as the Mexican economy recovered from the financial crises of the 1980s and 1990s, job opportunities increased.

These changes do not mean that the demand for unauthorized labor is also in decline. Since about 2008, the total number of unauthorized immigrants in the United States has remained steady, hovering just a few hundred thousand above or below eleven million. Even as the number of Mexican immigrants has declined, they have been replaced by people from other parts of the world. Between 2008 and 2021, the unauthorized population from Africa grew by 68 percent, from the Caribbean by 67 percent, from Central America by 52 percent, and from Asia by 47 percent.

We do not advocate for open borders or the end of immigration enforcement. However, the law must be updated. U.S. immigration law has not been significantly revised for over three decades, and it is severely misaligned with the nation's needs.[33] For example, there is significantly greater demand for immigrants in some industries, such as construction, health care, and hospitality, than there are available slots for legal immigrants. Such misalignment led to severe labor shortages during the recovery from the COVID-19 pandemic in 2021. Additionally, because current immigration law caps the number of immigrant admissions from each country at 7 percent of the world total, the wait time for those seeking to join a family member in the United States can be very long and inequitable. For example, a recent analysis by the Cato Institute projected that a Mexican national who qualified for admission under the F1 family preference category in 2018 (as an adult child of a U.S. citizen) would have to wait *thirty-nine years* before admission, and 15 percent would die before that day arrived.[34] By comparison, Filipinos in the same situation would need to wait eleven years, and 2.5 percent would die before admission. Finally, those from other countries would need to wait only six years, and 1.5 percent would die while on the waitlist.[35] Given the lengthy and inequitable wait times, it is understandable that people would be tempted to skirt the law to reunite with family members. We do not delve into specific policy solutions here, but nonpartisan groups such as Brookings and the Migration Policy Institute have developed well-reasoned and practical roadmaps for reform that warrant attention.[36]

It is also important to provide legal protections to the 11.2 million people who are currently working and living in this country without legal status. Sixty percent have been living in the country for a decade or more. They have put down roots, and many have U.S.-born children and grandchildren. One possibility is to grant legal permanent residency to targeted groups, such as childhood arrivals ("Dreamers"), those currently with Temporary Protected Status (TPS), parents of U.S.-born children, and those on the wait-list for family reunification. Another potential solution suggested by historian Mae Ngai is to impose a statute of limitations on immigration violations, as is currently the practice for minor crimes and misdemeanors committed by U.S. citizens.[37]

The Leveling Effects of Schooling

The third lesson from our research is that expansions in schooling and other opportunities have helped level the playing field. Richard Alba refers to such expansions as "non-zero-sum," because they potentially allow all groups to advance together.[38] With such expansions, no one must lose for others to gain. As we showed in chapter 5, compulsory public schooling in a well-funded school system tends to have a leveling effect on opportunity. In this context, parental education and background are far less determinative of a child's success. Children from poor families and children from rich families can be equally successful. This can be clearly seen in the experiences of Jenny's grandparents, George and Grace Mulder, who grew up in poor families but benefited from the well-funded public schools in Grand Rapids, Michigan. Italian immigrants had a similar experience. They arrived with less education than all other European immigrants. However, they settled in the northeastern and midwestern regions of the United States, places with well-developed public schools. Their children still fell behind somewhat, but their grandchildren exceeded native whites in education levels.

The promise of public schooling can also be seen in the experiences of Mexican Americans. The children of those who left Texas or attended better-funded schools during the Industrial Era had outcomes that looked a lot like those seen for Italians. As we showed in chapter 6, the reforms of the Civil Rights Era (accomplished in large part through the efforts of Mexican American–led social movements) and the equity-based policy changes that forced schools to attend to the specific needs of Mexican American children, such as No Child Left Behind, led to large improvements in education levels among later-vintage Mexican Americans. The second-generation children of immigrants who arrived during the latter half of the twentieth century went further in school and appear to be on a much more favorable upward trajectory than those from the earlier vintage.

The takeaway is that equity-based practices seem to be particularly effective in promoting integration and fostering social mobility. Children of immigrants need tailored instruction to bring them from wherever they start (regardless of their family background) to the level of expectations for other students. They also need equal access to quality schools. To move toward a more prosperous and equitable future, policies should be promoted that expand opportunities for all. We have seen that expanded access to K-12 schooling increased opportunities and promoted immigrant integration in the past. It is important now to expand access to both pre-K and postsecondary schooling. Many Hispanic children and children of immigrants are insufficiently prepared for elementary school because they have not attended preschool.[39] Universal pre-K programs could promote and equalize school readiness.[40] Also, postsecondary schooling has become essential in today's labor market, but the barriers faced by poor families remain formidable.[41] It will be important to make college more affordable or to provide tuition-free community college or other types of vocational training.[42] Because of the 2023 Supreme Court *SFFA v. Harvard* and *SFFA v. UNC* decisions, race-based affirmative action in college and university admissions is no longer permitted.[43] Alternative programs that target students who come from disadvantaged backgrounds or who are first-generation college students are unlikely to completely substitute for affirmative action, but they could help.[44] Like programs that expanded access for (nearly) all in the past, such as compulsory K-12 schooling, these initiatives could garner widespread support.

Third-Generation Delay Is an Artifact of Time and Place

The fourth lesson of our study is that the phenomenon of "third-generation delay" is an artifact of Mexican Americans' exclusion from educational opportunity in Texas prior to the Civil Rights Era. Recall from chapter 2 that third-generation delay is a pattern seen in cross-sectional data whereby the educational attainment of Mexican Americans increases between the first and second generations, but progress appears to stall between the second and third-and-later generations. Our research shows that third-generation delay is a pattern of mobility produced by historical factors that are obscured in present-day data and cross-sectional methods of analysis. It is *not* an indicator of present-day immigrant integration dynamics, and we urge immigration experts, analysts, and policymakers to avoid invoking the pattern as a basis for restricting immigration. Rather, the inability of early-vintage Mexican Americans to reach parity in educational attainment with white Americans serves as a *historical* lesson about the intergenerational consequences of excluding disadvantaged groups from the opportunity structure.

Furthermore, our data and analyses highlight for researchers the myriad risks of bias involved when cross-sectional data and methods are employed to study immigrant integration, a process that has unfolded over time and through distinct periods of American history. Cross-sections of contemporary data blind us to the experiences endured by the grandparents and great-grandparents of today's third and later Mexican American generations. This makes it impossible to assess the extent to which present-day educational disadvantages stem from those earlier periods. Census projects linking historical and contemporary census and survey data are now making it possible for the field of immigration research to begin reducing its reliance on cross-sectional data.

Conclusion

In closing, we want to reemphasize a point we made in the first chapter, namely, that the integration of Mexican immigrants is a test case for assessing whether America can successfully integrate poor and nonwhite immigrants into its middle-class mainstream in the same way it integrated the Industrial Era European immigrants.

Can it?

For middle- and late-vintage Mexican Americans, we are guardedly optimistic. Given the recent decline in unauthorized migration from Mexico and the more favorable educational advancement among the later vintages, we suspect that they will eventually be integrated into the American society and economy. That said, it will be important to continue to expand access to higher education, especially as the cost of higher education continues to rise, putting a college degree out of reach for many young adults.

However, we will continue to see challenges for early-vintage Mexican Americans. Our results indicate that the racialization of Mexican Americans was most intense in Jim Crow Era Texas, which produced, by design, massive gaps in educational attainment between whites and nonwhites. Unfortunately, these past disadvantages have persisted into the third generation. It is also difficult to be optimistic about the next group of immigrants who are likely to replace Mexicans as a source of low-cost labor, such as Central Americans. In their case, the nation seems poised to repeat the mistakes of the past. Pundits, policymakers, and some academics continue to underestimate the contributions that immigrants are likely to make in the future. In addition, politicians have little incentive to develop practical solutions to deal with unauthorized immigration. Instead, they continue to use it as a wedge issue to generate anger and fear among their constituents.

Still, pessimists about immigration typically have been wrong in the past. As two social scientists committed to studying these data, we would like to leave you with three reasons to be hopeful.

First, the American economy will soon be entering a period of transition and expansion. As Dowell Myers writes about in his book *Immigrants and Boomers*, the Baby Boom Generation is retiring, leaving job vacancies and creating demand for labor in hospitality, construction, and health care. In the green economy, with renewable energy installations and other big infrastructure projects also advancing, opportunities at all skill levels of the labor market are likely to expand. As in past periods of expansion, such as during and following World War II, openings in the new twenty-first-century labor market could enable a "non-zero-sum" expansion in opportunity whereby all groups are able to advance, including the children of poor immigrants.[45]

Second, the Baby Boom Generation will soon be replaced by a younger, more progressive generation. More than half (50.2 percent) of those born since 1990 are members of a nonwhite minority group, compared with 30.1 percent of Baby Boomers (born between 1946 and 1964). Moreover, 30 percent of those born since 1990 grew up in immigrant families, compared with 20 percent of Baby Boomers. Today's young adults are much more comfortable with mixed and fluid gender and racial identities, and they are more progressive in their views about race, multiculturalism, and gender equality.[46] Like the Progressives of the early twentieth century and the Latinos and African Americans who organized and protested during the civil rights movement of the 1960s, they may be willing to advocate for policies that aim to reform immigration policy or expand access to pre-K and postsecondary education.

Third, and perhaps most important, Mexican Americans and other Latinos continue to work diligently to improve opportunities and outcomes for Latin American immigrants and their children. In chapter 6, we described state and local Latino organizations protesting, attending school board meetings to advocate for bilingual instruction, and bringing cases before the Supreme Court in efforts to equalize funding formulas, reduce school segregation, and improve their children's and grandchildren's educational opportunities. Such efforts were sustained for decades, and they continue to this day, even in places that have resisted the sociocultural changes brought on by immigration.

This is evident in Holland, Michigan, where Jenny grew up. As described in the preface, Holland was transformed over the last fifty years from a Dutch immigrant enclave into a new destination for Mexican immigrants, and these changes were not always welcomed by the area's Dutch community. Yet one local Latino-led organization, Latin Americans United for Progress (LAUP), has been responding to the needs of the Mexican American community since 1975.[47] Supported by local businesses, private donors, grants, and volunteers, LAUP is the oldest Latino-led and Latino-serving organization in the state of Michigan. Like the Progressive Era programs provided by the American Seating Company, where Jenny's grandfather worked, LAUP offers a wide range of programs and services that help immigrants learn English, gain citizenship, secure home loans, promote health, fight discrimination, and connect with coethnics at cultural events. In recognition of the growing need for postsecondary education, LAUP also promotes young adults' access to higher education by mentoring youth, organizing college visits for high school students, and assisting families with college and financial aid applications. LAUP does not work alone: it is a member of the Hispanic Federation, a large national network composed of over six hundred nonprofit organizations that seek to strengthen local Latino communities.

LAUP's efforts march ahead despite political opposition. Following a presentation at a Holland-area church, LAUP's CEO, Johnny Rodriguez, was asked how his organization was impacted when a group of newly elected far-right politicians eliminated the county's Diversity, Equity and Inclusion (DEI) Department. Rodriguez responded with a quote from rapper Lil Wayne: "Real Gs move in silence like lasagna." He elaborated that LAUP does not attempt to engage in pointless political arguments. Rather, like the silent *g* in "lasagna," the organization works quietly and constructively with local employers, who "were the biggest drivers of that DEI department at the county level," to reduce discrimination in the workplace.[48]

The United States is a more vibrant, more prosperous, and culturally richer society because of immigration, but it has also struggled with a long history of structural racism, which has had long-lasting negative impacts on Mexican Americans today and could negatively impact the next immigrant groups recruited to take their places in American fields, kitchens, construction sites, and health care facilities. Like Industrial Era immigrants, today's immigrants need settlement assistance and equal access to opportunities to become successfully integrated into mainstream American society.

Despite some setbacks, we remain hopeful about the future, though not necessarily because we think structural racism will disappear or that Americans will voluntarily do the right thing (although many will). Rather, structural changes are coming. The new green economy and the aging of the Baby Boom Generation are likely to create demand for an expanded and highly educated workforce, and a majority of the young adults who will fill those jobs are members of ethnoracial minority groups. This means that future labor force needs are unlikely to be met without active efforts to promote postsecondary education among young Mexican Americans and other Latinos. Business groups seem ready to engage in these efforts, and Latino-led advocacy groups, like the *g* in "lasagna," will be there to push the nation in this direction.

~ Notes ~

Chapter 1. Digging into the Archives

1. National Opinion Research Center 2020.
2. Edmonston and Passel 1992.
3. Carlson and Carlson 1981.
4. "Generational status" is an indicator of the amount of time—measured in generations—that a person's family has lived in the United States. Immigrants compose the first generation, U.S.-born children with at least one immigrant parent make up the second generation, U.S.-born children with at least one immigrant grandparent (but no immigrant parents) make up the third generation, and so on.
5. Pew Research Center 2018a.
6. Ekins and Kemp 2021.
7. U.S. Office of the Interior 1928.
8. Pierce 1931.
9. American Seating Company 1938.
10. Ibid. 1919, 1923b.
11. Ibid. 1922b.
12. Ibid. 1922a,1923a.
13. Guarino 2016.
14. Gordon 1961, 279.
15. Hochschild and Mollenkopf 2008; Putnam 2007.
16. Perlmann 2005.
17. Myers 2007.
18. Lopez and Stanton-Salazar 2001; Portes and Rumbaut 2001; Waldinger and Feliciano 2004.
19. Perlmann 2005.
20. National Academies of Sciences, Engineering, and Medicine 2015.
21. Camarota 2001; Douthat 2013; Grogger and Trejo 2002; Huntington 2004.

https://doi.org/10.7758/fhka5464.9820

22. Portes and Zhou 1993.
23. Bean, Brown, and Bachmeier 2015.
24. Camarota 2001; Wojtkiewicz and Donato 1995; Zsembik and Llanes 1996.
25. Abramitzky and Boustan 2022.
26. Telles and Ortiz 2009.
27. Alexander et al. 2015.
28. Baker et al. 2011.
29. Montejano 1987.

Chapter 2. Mexican Americans as a Bellwether of Post-Industrial Integration

1. Gordon 1964.
2. Waters 1990.
3. Lieberson 1980.
4. Sugrue 1996/2005.
5. Kasarda 1989; Massey and Denton 1993.
6. Hirschman and Massey 2008.
7. Ruggles et al., 2024.
8. Alba and Nee 1997, 2003.
9. Kasinitz et al. 2008.
10. Alba and Nee 2003; Bean and Stevens 2003; Perlmann 2005.
11. Bonilla-Silva 1997.
12. Telles and Ortiz 2009.
13. Fox and Guglielmo 2012.
14. Portes and Zhou 1993.
15. Portes and Rumbaut 2001.
16. Wilson 1978, 1987.
17. Moore and Pinderhughes 1993.
18. Alba, Jiménez, and Marrow 2014; Jiménez and Fitzgerald 2007; Jiménez, Park, and Pedroza 2018.
19. Hirschman 2004, 388.
20. Ibid., 389.
21. Barrett 1992; Olneck 1989.
22. Douthat 2013.
23. Portes and Zhou 1993.
24. Borjas 1990.
25. Huntington 2004, 30.
26. Grogger and Trejo 2002.
27. Park and Myers 2010.
28. Alba, Jiménez, and Marrow 2014; Alvarez 1971, 1973; Jiménez 2010; Jiménez and Fitzgerald 2007; Waters and Jiménez 2005.
29. In a simulation based on actual age-specific fertility, mortality, and re-

turn migration rates, we followed each individual and their descendants over time, modeling whether they returned to Mexico or stayed in the United States, how many children they had, and when they died.

30. Waters 1990.
31. Duncan and Trejo 2011, 2018; Duncan et al. 2020; Antman, Duncan, and Trejo 2020.
32. Alexander et al. 2015.
33. Leach, Van Hook, and Bachmeier 2018; Massey et al. 2018; Wagner and Layne 2014.
34. For more details, see online supplement 2.2.
35. See online supplement 2.1.
36. This includes the Bracero Program Era, when large numbers of temporary agricultural workers from Mexico entered the United States between 1942 and 1964.
37. These sample sizes are small because not everyone can be linked across the years. The 1940 census data contain a record for everyone in the population, but the other data sources are large sample surveys. Thus, only a small subset of those in the 1940 census (but still a large absolute number) can be linked to the CPS data. Likewise, only a sample of those in the CPS can be linked to records in the Census 2000 long-form data or the ACS data. There are some small differences in the characteristics of those who are linked and those who are not. These differences do not appear to cause any significant bias in our results. Nevertheless, we adjusted for these differences out of caution, using a procedure called "inverse probability weighting," which essentially rebalances the linked sample so that it matches the full population. See online supplement 2.3 for more details.
38. U.S. Department of Education 2023.
39. See also Southern Education Foundation 2009.
40. Perlmann 2005.

Chapter 3. From the Tenements to the Top

1. Ruggles et al. 2024.
2. Cinel 2002; Gabaccia 2013.
3. Goldstein 1969; Perlmann 1988.
4. Hirschman and Mogford 2009; Kim 2007.
5. Alba 1990.
6. Riis 1890.
7. Hutchinson 1956.
8. Benton-Cohen 2018.
9. Downes 2011.
10. Benton-Cohen 2010.
11. Blau and Duncan 1967; Haller and Portes 1973.

12. Gratton and Moen 2004.
13. Montejano 1987; Taylor 1934.
14. Catron 2016.
15. Gans 2017.
16. Alexander 1962.
17. Foner 2013.
18. Gallup Organization 1939.
19. Foner 2013.
20. Cichon 2018.
21. Portes and Zhou 1993.
22. Alba and Nee 2003; Alexander 1962; Foner 2000; Higham 1956.
23. Gans 1979.
24. Waters 1990.
25. Alba 1981, 1985.
26. Glazer and Moynihan 1970.
27. Borjas 1994.
28. Borjas 1990; Borjas and Tienda 1987.
29. Portes and Rumbaut 2014; Waters, Ueda, and Marrow 2007.
30. Davis and Shear 2020; Douthat 2013.
31. Ran Abramitzky and Leah Boustan's book *Streets of Gold* (2022) makes a significant contribution by following immigrant families from the first to the second generation for both Industrial Era and contemporary immigrants. However, their data exclude women and Mexicans from the Industrial Era and do not follow immigrant families across three generations.
32. Waters 1990.
33. Lowrey et al. 2021. This article uses IGENS-20 data to examine intergenerational mobility among European Industrial Era immigrants and their descendants. It differs from the results presented in chapter 3 in that it presents results for families while chapter 3 presents results for individuals. Nevertheless, the mobility patterns are very similar.
34. Fischer and Hout 2006.
35. Haller and Portes 1973; Galobardes et al. 2006.
36. Kaplan, Fang, and Kirby 2017; Lynch 2003; Mirowsky and Ross 2003; Montez, Hummer, and Hayward 2012; Halpern-Manners et al. 2020.
37. Dubow, Boxer, and Huesmann 2009; Erola, Jalonen, and Lehti 2016; Vollmer et al. 2017.
38. Baldassarri and Abascal 2020; Duncan and Duncan 1968; Fischer and Hout 2006.
39. Additional information on high school, postsecondary schooling, and college completion can be found in online supplement 3.1.
40. Among adults ages twenty-five to sixty-four in the 2019 American Community Survey, African Americans had an average of 13.2 years of education, while non-Hispanic whites had attained 14.1 years—a difference of 0.9 years.

41. Fischer and Hout 2006.
42. Blau and Duncan 1967; Featherman 1971; Featherman and Hauser 1978.
43. Dubow, Boxer, and Huesmann 2009; Duncan and Brooks-Gunn 1997; Haveman and Smeeding 2006; McLoyd 1998.
44. More details about how we did this are provided in online supplement 3.2.
45. Abramitzky et al. 2021.
46. For a review, see Crosnoe and López Turley 2011.
47. Alba 2020.
48. Kim and Rury 2007.
49. Katz 1976; Lleras-Muney and Shertzer 2015; Richardson 1980.
50. Center on Education Policy 2020.
51. Lleras-Muney and Shertzer 2015.
52. Meyer 1980; Olneck 1989.
53. Lleras-Muney 2002.
54. Hirschman 2013.
55. Lleras-Muney and Shertzer 2015.
56. Ibid.
57. *Fortune* 2015.
58. WETA Washington, D.C., and Ark Media 2015.
59. Feliciano and Lanuza 2017.
60. Gabaccia 2013.
61. Alba and Nee 2003; Borjas 2000.
62. White and Mullen 2016.
63. Baker 1999.
64. Baker 1992.
65. Gleason 1970; Lazerson 1977; Moore 1986.
66. Baker 1992.
67. Boyd 1989.
68. Catron 2016.
69. Hirschman 2013.
70. Louie 2012.
71. Kao and Tienda 1995.
72. Lee and Zhou 2015.
73. Steinberg 1981.
74. Alba 2020.
75. Fox and Guglielmo 2012.
76. Hirschman 2013.

Chapter 4: Texas-Style Exclusion

1. Fox and Guglielmo 2012.
2. U.S. Office of Immigration Statistics 2022.

3. Ruggles et al. 2024.
4. Sanchez 1993.
5. Ibid.
6. Ibid., 52.
7. Montejano 1987.
8. Massey et al. 1987.
9. Sanchez 1993, 52.
10. Ibid., 51.
11. Ibid., 211.
12. Bernard 2024.
13. Lee, Peri, and Yasenov 2022.
14. See online supplement 4.1 for estimates of return migration during this period and the impact of the repatriation campaign on the characteristics of the Mexican Americans who remained in the United States.
15. Fox and Guglielmo 2012.
16. Ngai 2006.
17. Alba 2005.
18. Massey and Denton 1993; Rothstein 2017.
19. Fox and Guglielmo 2012.
20. Ibid., 347.
21. Hirschman 2004.
22. Ibid., 389.
23. Ibid.
24. Montejano 1987.
25. Taylor 1930, 421.
26. Cortes 1980, 697–719.
27. Fox and Guglielmo 2012, 352.
28. Ruggles et al. 2024.
29. Foley 2010.
30. Montejano 1987.
31. Foley 2010.
32. For example, the consumer price index in 1940 hovered around 100 for both California cities (101.1 in Los Angeles, 98.5 in San Diego, 98.4 in Vallejo-Benicia) and Texas cities (101.2 in Houston, 97.2 in Corpus Christi, 98.3 in Dallas). Tobin and Clague 1949.
33. Montejano 1987, ch. 9.
34. Ibid., 200.
35. Ibid., 219.
36. Ibid., 191.
37. Ibid., 193.
38. Ibid., 192–93.
39. Foley 2010; Telles and Ortiz 2009.
40. Almaguer 1994.

41. Menchaca 1995.
42. Sanchez 1993.
43. Almaguer 1994.
44. Sanchez 1993.
45. Ibid., 94.
46. Telles and Ortiz 2009.
47. Grebler, Moore, and Guzmán 1970.
48. The questions used by the Census Bureau today to identify persons of Mexican origin were first introduced into census surveys in the 1970s. Prior to that, the Mexican-origin population was approximated based on whether individuals were coded by census-takers as having a Spanish surname.
49. State of California 1924; State of Texas 1924.
50. Perlmann 2005.
51. We discuss this point in greater detail in online supplement 4.2.
52. Dubow, Boxer, and Huesmann 2009; Duncan and Brooks-Gunn 1997; Duncan et al. 1998; Duncan, Magnuson, and Votruba-Drzal 2017.
53. Bohon, Macpherson, and Atiles 2005; Fernandez, Paulsen, and Hirano-Nakanishi 1989; Ogbu 1987.
54. Vega 2014.
55. Ibid.
56. Jackson 2016.
57. Suhay, Tenenbaum, and Bartola 2022.
58. Borjas 1992, 2006; Duncan and Trejo 2015.
59. Fox and Guglielmo 2012.
60. See online supplement 3.3
61. See online supplement 4.4 for more information about how we did this analysis.
62. See online supplement 4.4.

Chapter 5: The Leveling Effects of Industrial Era School Expansion

1. Greene and Jacobs 1992; Katz 1976; Meyer et al. 1979.
2. Anderson 1955; Richardson 1980.
3. Greene and Jacobs 1992; Katz 1976; Meyer et al. 1979.
4. Richardson 1980; Tyack 1976.
5. Richardson 1984.
6. Massey and Denton 1993.
7. See online supplement 5.1 for more detail.
8. See online supplement 5.2 for the full models.

Chapter 6: A Fair Shot

1. Biden 2020.
2. Tesch and Editors of Encyclopaedia Britannica 2014; Montejano 1987.
3. Montejano 1987.
4. Kibbe 1946, 17.
5. Montejano 1987.
6. Ibid.
7. Brown v. Board of Education, 347 U.S. 483 (1954).
8. U.S. Government 1964.
9. U.S. Commission on Civil Rights 1965.
10. U.S. Commission on Civil Rights 2001.
11. The Fair Housing Act, Pub. L. No. 42, 3601–3619 U.S.C. (1968).
12. Fox and Guglielmo 2012.
13. Montejano 1987.
14. Hernandez v. Texas, 347 U.S. 475 (1954).
15. Kratz 2021.
16. Capps, Fix, and Batalova 2020; Lowrey and Van Hook 2021.
17. Montejano 1987.
18. Donato 1997; Garth 1926; Sanchez 1932.
19. M. Mendez v. Westminister School Dist., 64 F. Supp. 544 (S.D. Cal. 1946).
20. Montejano 1987.
21. Kilgarlin v. Martin, 252 F. Supp. 404 (S.D. Tex. 1966).
22. Donato 1997.
23. We do not extend the results to 2020 because of apparent changes in the way data on ethnoracial background were collected, leading to an abrupt single-year change in school segregation in California between 2015 and 2016.
24. Logan and Stults 2021, 2022.
25. Passel 2005.
26. Garip and Asad 2016; Logan, Zhang, and Alba 2002.
27. Brown 2007.
28. Agius Vallejo 2012.
29. Fix and Capps 2005.
30. Donato 1997.
31. Chavez and Partida 2020.
32. Isensee 2015.
33. Del Rio ISD v. Salvatierra, 33 S.W.2d 790 (Tex. Civ. App. 1930). Note that the large funding gap between school districts had to do with not just the way the state legislature apportioned funding but also the use of local property tax revenues to subsidize schools. The property values and tax rates that determined expenditures were different in the two districts.
34. Isensee 2015.

35. San Antonio School District v. Rodriguez, 411 U.S. 1 (1973).
36. Edgewood v. Kirby, Pub. L. No. 777 S.W.2d 391, TX (1989).
37. Isensee 2015.
38. Chira 1992.
39. Ibid.
40. Donato 1997, 109.
41. Chavez and Partida 2020; Serna v. Portales, 351 F. Supp. 1279 (D.N.M. 1972).
42. Lau v. Nichols, 414 U.S. 563 (1974).
43. Texas Education Agency 2000.
44. U.S. Department of Education, n.d.
45. Lazarin 2022.
46. Mintz 2000.
47. Dee and Jacob 2010.
48. Lauen and Gaddis 2012; Springer 2008.
49. Lazarin 2022, 1.
50. The estimates are adjusted for basic demographic factors (sex, birth cohort, family size, region of residence), but the results are very similar regardless of whether we made these adjustments.
51. See online supplement 6.1.
52. See online supplement 6.2.
53. Methodological details are provided in online supplement 4.2.
54. See online supplement 6.3.

Chapter 7: Building New Walls

1. Mitchell 2010.
2. Mitchell 2016.
3. Myers 2007.
4. U.S. Bureau of the Census 2023.
5. Passel and Cohn 2017.
6. Hajnal 2021; Parker 2021.
7. U.S. Bureau of the Census 2023.
8. Borjas 1990.
9. Davis and Shear 2020.
10. Gelatt 2017.
11. Lowrey and Van Hook 2021.
12. Martin 2019, italics added.
13. Fortuny and Chaudry 2011.
14. Capps, Fix, and Henderson 2009; Van Hook and Bean 2009.
15. Duncan and Horton 2020; Ro et al. 2023; Bernstein, Gonzalez, and Karpman 2021.
16. Garcia et al. 2021.
17. Noori Farzan 2019.

18. Massey, Durand, and Malone 2002; Massey, Durand, and Pren 2015.
19. Passel and Cohn 2009; Reyes 2001, 2004; Rosenblum et al. 2012.
20. Van Hook, Gelatt, and Ruiz Soto 2023.
21. Hall and Greenman 2013.
22. Plyler v. Doe, 457 U.S. 202 (1982).
23. National Immigration Law Center 2023.
24. Dreby 2010, 2015.
25. Amuedo-Dorantes and Arenas-Arroyo 2018, 2019.
26. Allen, Cisneros, and Tellez 2015; Bean, Brown, and Bachmeier 2015; Brabeck, Sibley, and Lykes 2016; Lu, He, and Brooks-Gunn 2020; Yoshikawa and Kalil 2011.
27. Dreby 2012.
28. Berger Cardoso et al. 2018; Dreby 2015; Enriquez 2015; Yoshikawa 2011.
29. Enriquez 2015.
30. Bean, Brown, and Bachmeier 2015.
31. Radde 2023.
32. Valdes 2023.
33. Chishti, Gelatt, and Meissner 2021.
34. Bier 2019.
35. Gelatt 2019.
36. Bahar and Wright 2023; Chishti, Gelatt, and Meissner 2021.
37. Ngai 2004.
38. Alba 2020.
39. Magnuson, Lahaie, and Waldfogel 2006.
40. Garcia and Jensen 2007.
41. Baum and Flores 2011.
42. Batalova and Fix 2022.
43. Students for Fair Admissions, Inc. v. President and Fellows of Harvard College, 600 U.S. ___ (2023); *Students for Fair Admissions, Inc. v. University of North Carolina*, 1:14CV954 (M.D.N.C. Sep. 30, 2019).
44. Harris and Tienda 2010, 2012.
45. Alba 2020.
46. Pew Research Center 2018b.
47. For more information, see the Latin Americans United for Progress website (https://laup.org/.)
48. Hope Church Adult Education 2024.

~ References ~

Abramitzky, Ran, and Leah Boustan. 2022. *Streets of Gold: America's Untold Story of Immigrant Success.* New York: Public Affairs.

Abramitzky, Ran, Leah Boustan, Elisa Jácome, and Santiago Pérez. 2021. "Intergenerational Mobility of Immigrants in the United States over Two Centuries." *American Economic Review* 111(2, February 1): 580–608. https://doi.org/10.1257/aer.20191586.

Agius Vallejo, Jody. 2012. *Barrios to Burbs: The Making of the Mexican American Middle Class.* Stanford, Calif.: Stanford University Press.

Alba, Richard. 1981. "The Twilight of Ethnicity among American Catholics of European Ancestry." *Annals of the American Academy of Political and Social Science* 454(1): 86–97.

———. 1985. "The Twilight of Ethnicity among Americans of European Ancestry: The Case of Italians." *Ethnic and Racial Studies* 8(1, January): 134–58. https://doi.org/10.1080/01419870.1985.9993478.

———. 1990. *Ethnic Identity: The Transformation of White America.* New Haven, Conn.: Yale University Press.

———. 2005. "Bright vs. Blurred Boundaries: Second-Generation Assimilation and Exclusion in France, Germany, and the United States." *Ethnic and Racial Studies* 28(1, January): 20–49. https://doi.org/10.1080/0141987042000280003.

———. 2020. *The Great Demographic Illusion: Majority, Minority, and the Expanding American Mainstream.* Princeton, N.J.: Princeton University Press.

Alba, Richard, Tomás R. Jiménez, and Helen B. Marrow. 2014. "Mexican Americans as a Paradigm for Contemporary Intra-Group Heterogeneity." *Ethnic and Racial Studies* 37(3, February 23): 446–66. https://doi.org/10.1080/01419870.2013.786111.

Alba, Richard, and Victor Nee. 1997. "Rethinking Assimilation Theory for a New Era of Immigration." *International Migration Review* 31(4): 826–74.

————. 2003. *Remaking the American Mainstream: Assimilation and Contemporary Immigration.* Cambridge, Mass.: Harvard University Press.

Alexander, Charles C. 1962. "Prophet of American Racism: Madison Grant and the Nordic Myth." *Phylon* 23(1): 73–90. https://doi.org/10.2307/274146.

Alexander, J. Trent, Todd Gardner, Catherine G. Massey, and Amy O'Hara. 2015. "Creating a Longitudinal Data Infrastructure at the Census Bureau." U.S. Bureau of the Census, May 1. https://www.census.gov/content/dam/Census/library/working-papers/2015/adrm/2015-alexander.pdf.

Allen, Brian, Erica M. Cisneros, and Alexandra Tellez. 2015. "The Children Left Behind: The Impact of Parental Deportation on Mental Health." *Journal of Child and Family Studies* 24(2, February): 386–92. https://doi.org/10.1007/s10826-013-9848-5.

Almaguer, Tomas. 1994. *Racial Fault Lines: The Historical Origins of White Supremacy in California.* Berkeley: University of California Press.

Alvarez, Rodolfo. 1971. "The Unique Psycho-Historical Experience of the Mexican-American People." *Social Science Quarterly* 52(1): 15–29.

————. 1973. "The Psycho-Historical and Socioeconomic Development of the Chicano Community in the United States." *Social Science Quarterly* 53(4): 920–42.

American Seating Company. 1919. "Americanization." *Seater*, November.

————. 1922a. "Night Schools." *Seater*, November.

————. 1922b. "Program of Self-Education." *Seater*, December.

————. 1923a. "Contribute to Illiteracy." *Seater*, July.

————. 1923b. "Seaters Become 93% American as These Men Get Papers." *Seater*, October.

————. 1938. "Made for Modern Schools." *Seater*, February.

Amuedo-Dorantes, Catalina, and Esther Arenas-Arroyo. 2018. "Split Families and the Future of Children: Immigration Enforcement and Foster Care Placements." *AEA Papers and Proceedings* 108: 368–72.

————. 2019. "Immigration Enforcement and Children's Living Arrangements." *Journal of Policy Analysis and Management* 38(1, Winter): 11–40. https://doi.org/10.1002/pam.22106.

Anderson, C. Arnold. 1955. "Inequalities in Schooling in the South." *American Journal of Sociology* 60(6): 547–61.

Antman, Francisca M., Brian Duncan, and Stephen J. Trejo. 2020. "Ethnic Attrition, Assimilation, and the Measured Health Outcomes of Mexican Americans." *Journal of Population Economics* 33(4, October): 1499–1522. https://doi.org/10.1007/s00148-020-00772-8.

Bahar, Dany, and Greg Wright. 2023. "A Roadmap for Immigration Reform: Identifying Weak Links in the Labor Supply Chain." Brookings, March 27. https://www.brookings.edu/articles/a-roadmap-for-immigration-reform/.

Baker, David P. 1992. "The Politics of American Catholic School Expansion,

1870–1930." In Baker, *The Political Construction of Education: The State, School Expansion, and Economic Change.* New York: Praeger.

———. 1999. "Schooling All the Masses: Reconsidering the Origins of American Schooling in the Postbellum Era." *Sociology of Education* 72(4, October): 197. https://doi.org/10.2307/2673153.

Baker, David P., Juan Leon, Emily G. Smith Greenaway, John Collins, and Marcela Movit. 2011. "The Education Effect on Population Health: A Reassessment." *Population and Development Review* 37(2): 307–32.

Baldassarri, Delia, and Maria Abascal. 2020. "Diversity and Prosocial Behavior." *Science* 369(6508, September 4): 1183–87. https://doi.org/10.1126/science.abb2432.

Barrett, James R. 1992. "Americanization from the Bottom Up: Immigration and the Remaking of the Working Class in the United States, 1880–1930." *Journal of American History* 79(3): 996–1020. https://doi.org/10.2307/2080796.

Batalova, Jeanne, and Michael Fix. 2022. "Diverging Pathways: Immigrants' Legal Status and Access to Postsecondary Credentials." Migration Policy Institute, October. https://www.migrationpolicy.org/sites/default/files/publications/mpi-postsecondary-credentials-immigration-status_final.pdf.

Baum, Sandy, and Stella M. Flores. 2011. "Higher Education and Children in Immigrant Families." *The Future of Children* 21(1): 171–93.

Bean, Frank D., Susan K. Brown, and James D. Bachmeier. 2015. *Parents without Papers: The Progress and Pitfalls of Mexican American Integration.* New York: Russell Sage Foundation.

Bean, Frank D., and Gillian Stevens. 2003. *America's Newcomers and the Dynamics of Diversity.* New York: Russell Sage Foundation.

Benton-Cohen, Katherine. 2010. "The Rude Birth of Immigration Reform." *Wilson Quarterly* 34(3): 16–22.

———. 2018. *Inventing the Immigration Problem: The Dillingham Commission and Its Legacy.* Cambridge, Mass.: Harvard University Press.

Berger Cardoso, Jodi, Jennifer L. Scott, Monica Faulkner, and Liza Barros Lane. 2018. "Parenting in the Context of Deportation Risk." *Journal of Marriage and Family* 80(2, April): 301–16. https://doi.org/10.1111/jomf.12463.

Bernard, Diane. 2024. "The President Who Deported 1 Million Mexican Americans Nearly a Century Ago." *Washington Post,* February 21. https://www.washingtonpost.com/history/2024/02/21/herbert-hoover-deportation-immigration-trump/.

Bernstein, Hamutal, Dulce Gonzalez, and Michael Karpman. 2021. "Adults in Low-Income Immigrant Families Were Deeply Affected by the COVID-19 Crisis yet Avoided Safety Net Programs in 2020." Urban Institute, https://www.urban.org/research/publication/adults-low-income-immigrant-families-were-deeply-affected-covid-19-crisis-yet-avoided-safety-net-programs-2020.

Biden, Joseph. 2020. "Joe Biden Roundtable on Economic Impact of CO-VID-19 Transcript December 2." *Rev*, December 2, 2020. https://www.rev
.com/blog/transcripts/joe-biden-roundtable-on-economic-impact-of-covid
-19-transcript-december-2.

Bier, David J. 2019. "Immigration Wait Times from Quotas Have Doubled: Green Card Backlogs Are Long, Growing, and Inequitable." Cato Institute, June 18. https://www.cato.org/publications/policy-analysis/immigration
-wait-times-quotas-have-doubled-green-card-backlogs-are-long.

Blau, Peter, and Otis Dudley Duncan. 1967. *The American Occupational Structure*. New York: Wiley.

Bohon, Stephanie A., Heather Macpherson, and Jorge H. Atiles. 2005. "Educational Barriers for New Latinos in Georgia." *Journal of Latinos and Education* 4(1, January): 43–58. https://doi.org/10.1207/s1532771xjle0401_4.

Bonilla-Silva, Eduardo. 1997. "Rethinking Racism: Toward a Structural Interpretation." *American Sociological Review* 62(3): 465–80. https://doi
.org/10.2307/2657316.

Borjas, George J. 1990. *Friends or Strangers: The Impact of Immigrants on the U.S. Economy*. New York: Basic Books.

———. 1992. "National Origin and the Skills of Immigrants in the Postwar Period." In Borjas, *Immigration and the Work Force: Economic Consequences for the United States and Source Areas*. Chicago: University of Chicago Press.

———. 1994. "Long-Run Convergence of Ethnic Skill Differentials: The Children and Grandchildren of the Great Migration." *Industrial and Labor Relations Review* 47(4): 553–73. https://doi.org/10.2307/2524658.

———. 2000. "Ethnic Enclaves and Assimilation." *Swedish Economic Policy Review* 89(122): 89–122.

———. 2006. "Making It in America: Social Mobility in the Immigrant Population." *The Future of Children* 16(2, Fall): 55–71. https://doi.org
/10.1353/foc.2006.0013.

Borjas, George J., and Marta Tienda. 1987. "The Economic Consequences of Immigration." *Science* 235(4789): 645–51.

Boyd, Monica. 1989. "Family and Personal Networks in International Migration: Recent Developments and New Agendas." *International Migration Review* 23(3): 638–70. https://doi.org/10.2307/2546433.

Brabeck, Kalina M., Erin Sibley, and M. Brinton Lykes. 2016. "Authorized and Unauthorized Immigrant Parents: The Impact of Legal Vulnerability on Family Contexts." *Hispanic Journal of Behavioral Sciences* 38(1, February): 3–30. https://doi.org/10.1177/0739986315621741.

Brown, Susan K. 2007. "Delayed Spatial Assimilation: Multigenerational Incorporation of the Mexican-Origin Population in Los Angeles." *City and Community* 6(3, September): 193–209. https://doi.org/10.1111/j.1540
-6040.2007.00213.x.

Camarota, Steven A. 2001. "Immigration from Mexico: Assessing the Impact on the United States." CIS Paper 19. Center for Immigration Studies, July. https://cis.org/sites/cis.org/files/articles/2001/mexico/mexico.pdf.

Capps, Randy, Michael Fix, and Jeanne Batalova. 2020. "Anticipated 'Chilling Effects' of the Public-Charge Rule Are Real: Census Data Reflect Steep Decline in Benefits Use by Immigrant Families." Migration Policy Institute, December. https://www.migrationpolicy.org/news/anticipated-chilling-effects-public-charge-rule-are-real.

Capps, Randy, Michael E. Fix, and Everett Henderson. 2009. "Trends in Immigrants' Use of Public Assistance after Welfare Reform." In *Immigrants and Welfare: The Impact of Welfare Reform on America's Newcomers*, edited by Michael E. Fix. New York: Russell Sage Foundation.

Carlson, Mary C., and Robert L. Carlson. 1981. "The Country School and the Americanization of Ethnic Groups in North Dakota." Country School Legacy Project. Washington, D.C.: National Endowment for the Humanities.

Catron, Peter. 2016. "Made in America? Immigrant Occupational Mobility in the First Half of the Twentieth Century." *American Journal of Sociology* 122(2, September): 325–78. https://doi.org/10.1086/688043.

Center on Education Policy. 2020. "History and Evolution of Public Education in the U.S." Washington, D.C.: George Washington University, Graduate School of Education and Human Development.

Chavez, Herman Luis, and Maria Guadalupe Partida. 2020. "Research Guides: A Latinx Resource Guide: Civil Rights Cases and Events in the United States: 1968: East Los Angeles Walkouts." Washington, D.C.: Library of Congress, Hispanic Reading Room. https://guides.loc.gov/latinx-civil-rights/east-la-walkouts.

Chira, Susan. 1992. "The 1992 Campaign: Shaking the Schools; When Perot Took on Texas: A Special Report; Education Initiative Revealed a Savvy and Abrasive Perot." *New York Times*, June 29. https://www.nytimes.com/1992/06/29/us/1992-campaign-shaking-schools-when-perot-took-texas-special-report-education.html.

Chishti, Muzaffar, Julia Gelatt, and Doris Meissner. 2021. "Rethinking the U.S. Legal Immigration System: A Policy Road Map." Migration Policy Institute, May. https://www.migrationpolicy.org/research/rethinking-us-legal-immigration-road-map.

Cichon, Steve. 2018. "'Sht*hole Country' Is 2018 Speak for No Irish, No Colored, No Polish, No Italian. …" Buffalo Stories, January 12. http://blog.buffalostories.com/tag/no-italians-need-apply/.

Cinel, Dino. 2002. *The National Integration of Italian Return Migration, 1870–1929.* Cambridge: Cambridge University Press.

Cortes, Carlos E. 1980. "Mexicans." In *The Harvard Encyclopedia of American Ethnic Groups*, edited by Stephan Thernstrom. Cambridge, Mass.: Harvard University Press.

Crosnoe, Robert, and Ruth N. López Turley. 2011. "K-12 Educational Outcomes of Immigrant Youth." *The Future of Children* 21(1): 129–52.

Davis, Julie H., and Michael D. Shear. 2020. *Border Wars: Inside Trump's Assault on Immigration.* New York: Simon & Schuster.

Dee, Thomas S., and Brian A. Jacob. 2010. "The Impact of No Child Left Behind on Students, Teachers, and Schools." *Brookings Papers on Economic Activity* 2: 149–94.

Donato, Rubén. 1997. *The Other Struggle for Equal Schools: Mexican Americans during the Civil Rights Era.* New York: State University of New York Press.

Douthat, Ross. 2013. "When Assimilation Stalls." *New York Times*, April 27, 2013. https://www.nytimes.com/2013/04/28/opinion/sunday/douthat-when-the-assimilation-of-immigrants-stalls.html.

Downes, Lawrence. 2011. "One Hundred Years of Multitude." *New York Times*, March 26. https://www.nytimes.com/2011/03/26/opinion/26sat4.html.

Dreby, Joanna. 2010. *Divided by Borders: Mexican Migrants and Their Children.* Berkeley: University of California Press.

———. 2012. "The Burden of Deportation on Children in Mexican Immigrant Families." *Journal of Marriage and Family* 74(4, August): 829–45. https://doi.org/10.1111/j.1741-3737.2012.00989.x.

———. 2015. "U.S. Immigration Policy and Family Separation: The Consequences for Children's Well-being." *Social Science and Medicine* 132(May): 245–51. https://doi.org/10.1016/j.socscimed.2014.08.041.

Dubow, Eric F., Paul Boxer, and L. Rowell Huesmann. 2009. "Long-Term Effects of Parents' Education on Children's Educational and Occupational Success: Mediation by Family Interactions, Child Aggression, and Teenage Aspirations." *Merrill-Palmer Quarterly* 55(3, July): 224–49. https://doi.org/10.1353/mpq.0.0030.

Duncan, Beverly, and Otis Dudley Duncan. 1968. "Minorities and the Process of Stratification." *American Sociological Review* 33(3): 356–64.

Duncan, Brian, Jeffrey Grogger, Ana Sofia Leon, and Stephen J. Trejo. 2020. "New Evidence of Generational Progress for Mexican Americans." *Labour Economics* 62(January): 101771. https://doi.org/10.1016/j.labeco.2019.101771.

Duncan, Brian, and Stephen J. Trejo. 2011. "Intermarriage and the Intergenerational Transmission of Ethnic Identity and Human Capital for Mexican Americans." *Journal of Labor Economics* 29(2, April): 195–227. https://doi.org/10.1086/658088.

———. 2015. "Assessing the Socioeconomic Mobility and Integration of U.S. Immigrants and Their Descendants." *Annals of the American Academy of Political and Social Science* 657(1): 108–35. https://doi.org/10.1177/0002716214548396.

———. 2018. "Identifying the Later-Generation Descendants of U.S. Immigrants: Issues Arising from Selective Ethnic Attrition." *Annals of the Ameri-*

can Academy of Political and Social Science 677(1, May 1): 131–38. https://doi.org/10.1177/0002716218763293.

Duncan, Greg J., and Jeanne Brooks-Gunn, eds. 1997. *Consequences of Growing Up Poor.* New York: Russell Sage Foundation.

Duncan, Greg J., Katherine Magnuson, and Elizabeth Votruba-Drzal. 2017. "Moving beyond Correlations in Assessing the Consequences of Poverty." *Annual Review of Psychology* 68(1, January 3): 413–34. https://doi.org/10.1146/annurev-psych-010416-044224.

Duncan, Greg J., W. Jean Yeung, Jeanne Brooks-Gunn, and Judith R. Smith. 1998. "How Much Does Childhood Poverty Affect the Life Chances of Children?" *American Sociological Review* 63(3): 406–23. https://doi.org/10.2307/2657556.

Duncan, Whitney L., and Sarah B. Horton. 2020. "Serious Challenges and Potential Solutions for Immigrant Health during COVID-19." *Health Affairs Forefront*, April 18. https://doi.org/10.1377/forefront.20200416.887086.

Edmonston, Barry, and Jeffrey S. Passel. 1992. "Immigration and Immigrant Generations in Population Projections." *International Journal of Forecasting* 8(3, November): 459–76. https://doi.org/10.1016/0169-2070(92)90058-H.

Ekins, Emily, and David Kemp. 2021. "E Pluribus Unum: Findings from the Cato Institute 2021 Immigration and Identity National Survey." Washington, D.C.: Cato Institute, April 27. https://www.cato.org/survey-reports/e-pluribus-unum-findings-cato-institute-2021-immigration-identity-national-survey.

Enriquez, Laura E. 2015. "Multigenerational Punishment: Shared Experiences of Undocumented Immigration Status within Mixed-Status Families." *Journal of Marriage and Family* 77(4, August): 939–53. https://doi.org/10.1111/jomf.12196.

Erola, Jani, Sanni Jalonen, and Hannu Lehti. 2016. "Parental Education, Class, and Income over Early Life Course and Children's Achievement." *Research in Social Stratification and Mobility* 44(June): 33–43. https://doi.org/10.1016/j.rssm.2016.01.003.

Featherman, David L. 1971. "The Socioeconomic Achievement of White Religio-Ethnic Subgroups: Social and Psychological Explanations." *American Sociological Review* 36(2, April): 207–22. https://doi.org/10.2307/2094039.

Featherman, David L., and Robert M. Hauser. 1978. *Opportunity and Change.* New York: Academic Press.

Feliciano, Cynthia, and Yader R. Lanuza. 2017. "An Immigrant Paradox? Contextual Attainment and Intergenerational Educational Mobility." *American Sociological Review* 82(1, February): 211–41. https://doi.org/10.1177/0003122416684777.

Fernandez, Roberto M., Ronnelle Paulsen, and Marsha Hirano-Nakanishi.

1989. "Dropping Out among Hispanic Youth." *Social Science Research* 18(1, March): 21–52. https://doi.org/10.1016/0049-089X(89)90002-1.

Fischer, Claude S., and Michael Hout. 2006. *Century of Difference: How America Changed in the Last One Hundred Years.* New York: Russell Sage Foundation.

Fix, Michael, and Randy Capps. 2005. "Immigrant Children, Urban Schools, and the No Child Left Behind Act." Migration Policy Institute, November 1. https://www.migrationpolicy.org/article/immigrant-children-urban-schools-and-no-child-left-behind-act.

Foley, Neil. 2010. *Quest for Equality: The Failed Promise of Black-Brown Solidarity.* Cambridge, Mass.: Harvard University Press.

Foner, Nancy. 2000. *From Ellis Island to JFK: New York's Two Great Waves of Immigration.* New Haven, Conn.: Yale University Press.

———. 2013. "Immigration Past and Present." *Daedalus* 142(3, Summer): 16–25. https://doi.org/10.1162/DAED_a_00216.

Fortune. 2015. "Here's Fortune's Survey on How Americans Viewed Jewish Refugees in 1938." https://fortune.com/2015/11/18/fortune-survey-jewish-refugees/#jewish-refugees.

Fortuny, Karina, and Ajay Chaudry. 2011. "A Comprehensive Review of Immigrant Access to Health and Human Services." Urban Institute, June. https://www.urban.org/sites/default/files/publication/27651/412425-A-Comprehensive-Review-of-Immigrant-Access-to-Health-and-Human-Services.PDF.

Fox, Cybelle, and Thomas A. Guglielmo. 2012. "Defining America's Racial Boundaries: Blacks, Mexicans, and European Immigrants, 1890–1945." *American Journal of Sociology* 118(2): 327–79. https://doi.org/10.1086/666383.

Gabaccia, Donna R. 2013. *Italy's Many Diasporas.* New York: Routledge.

Gallup Organization. 1939. "Gallup Poll #1939-0169: Neutrality Law/World War II/1940 Presidential Election, Gallup Organization." Ithaca, N.Y.: Cornell University, Roper Center for Public Opinion Research.

Galobardes, Bruna, Mary Shaw, Debbie A. Lawlor, John W. Lynch, and George Davey Smith. 2006. "Indicators of Socioeconomic Position (Part 1)." *Journal of Epidemiology and Community Health* 60(1, January): 7–12. https://doi.org/10.1136/jech.2004.023531.

Gans, Herbert J. 1979. "Symbolic Ethnicity: The Future of Ethnic Groups and Cultures in America." *Ethnic and Racial Studies* 2(1): 1–20. https://doi.org/10.1080/01419870.1979.9993248.

———. 2017. "Racialization and Racialization Research." *Ethnic and Racial Studies* 40(3): 341–52.

Garcia, Erika, Sandrah P. Eckel, Zhanghua Chen, Kenan Li, and Frank D. Gilliland. 2021. "COVID-19 Mortality in California Based on Death Certificates: Disproportionate Impacts across Racial/Ethnic Groups and Nativity."

Annals of Epidemiology 58(June): 69–75. https://doi.org/10.1016/j.ann epidem.2021.03.006.

Garcia, Eugene E., and Bryant Jensen. 2007. "Advancing School Readiness for Young Hispanic Children through Universal Prekindergarten." *Harvard Journal of Hispanic Policy* 19: 25–37.

Garip, Filiz, and Asad L. Asad. 2016. "Network Effects in Mexico-U.S. Migration: Disentangling the Underlying Social Mechanisms." *American Behavioral Scientist* 60(10, September): 1168–93. https://doi.org/10.1177/00027 64216643131.

Garth, Thomas R. 1926. "Race and Psychology." *Scientific Monthly* 23(3): 240–45.

Gelatt, Julia. 2017. "The RAISE Act: Dramatic Change to Family Immigration, Less So for the Employment-Based System." Migration Policy Institute, August 4. https://www.migrationpolicy.org/news/raise-act-dramatic-change-family-immigration-less-so-employment-based-system.

———. 2019. "Explainer: How the U.S. Legal Immigration System Works." Washington, D.C.: Migration Policy Institute, April 26. https://www.migra tionpolicy.org/content/explainer-how-us-legal-immigration-system-works.

Glazer, Nathan, and Daniel P. Moynihan. 1970. *Beyond the Melting Pot: The Negroes, Puerto Ricans, Jews, Italians, and Irish of New York City.* Cambridge, Mass.: MIT Press.

Gleason, Phillip. 1970. "The Crisis of Americanization." In *Catholicism in America*, edited by Phillip Gleason. New York: Harper & Row.

Goldstein, Sidney. 1969. "Socioeconomic Differentials among Religious Groups in the United States." *American Journal of Sociology* 74(6): 612–31.

Gordon, Milton M. 1961. "Assimilation in America: Theory and Reality." *Daedalus* 90(2): 263–85.

———. 1964. *Assimilation in American Life: The Role of Race, Religion, and National Origins.* Oxford: Oxford University Press.

Gratton, Brian, and Jon Moen. 2004. "Immigration, Culture, and Child Labor in the United States, 1880–1920." *Journal of Interdisciplinary History* 34(3): 355–91.

Grebler, Leo, Joan Moore, and Ralph Guzmán. 1970. *The Mexican American People: The Nation's Second Largest Minority.* New York: Free Press.

Greene, Margaret E., and Jerry A. Jacobs. 1992. "Urban Enrollments and the Growth of Schooling: Evidence from the U.S. 1910 Census Public Use Sample." *American Journal of Education* 101(1): 29–59.

Grogger, Jeffrey, and Stephen J. Trejo. 2002. *Falling Behind or Moving Up? The Intergenerational Progress of Mexican Americans.* San Francisco: Public Policy Institute of California.

Guarino, Ben. 2016. "Famously Divisive 'Speak English' Sign Pulled from Philadelphia Cheesesteak Shop." *Washington Post*, October 17. https://www.washingtonpost.com/news/morning-mix/wp/2016/10/17/famously-divisive-speak-english-sign-pulled-from-philadelphia-cheesesteak-shop/.

Hajnal, Zoltan. 2021. "Immigration and the Origins of White Backlash." *Daedalus* 150(2, Spring): 23–39. https://doi.org/10.1162/daed_a_01844.

Hall, Matthew, and Emily Greenman. 2013. "Housing and Neighborhood Quality among Undocumented Mexican and Central American Immigrants." *Social Science Research* 42(6, November): 10.1016/j.ssresearch .2013.07.011. https://doi.org/10.1016/j.ssresearch.2013.07.011.

Haller, Archibald O., and Alejandro Portes. 1973. "Status Attainment Processes." *Sociology of Education* 46(1, Winter): 51–91. https://doi.org/10 .2307/2112205.

Halpern-Manners, Andrew, Jonas Helgertz, John Robert Warren, and Evan Roberts. 2020. "The Effects of Education on Mortality: Evidence from Linked U.S. Census and Administrative Mortality Data." *Demography* 57(4, August 1): 1513–41. https://doi.org/10.1007/s13524-020-00892-6.

Harris, Angel L., and Marta Tienda. 2010. "Minority Higher Education Pipeline: Consequences of Changes in College Admissions Policy in Texas." *Annals of the American Academy of Political and Social Science* 627(1): 60–81.

———. 2012. "Hispanics in Higher Education and the Texas Top 10% Law." *Race and Social Problems* 4(1, April): 57–67. https://doi.org/10.1007 /s12552-012-9065-7.

Haveman, Robert, and Timothy Smeeding. 2006. "The Role of Higher Education in Social Mobility." *The Future of Children* 16(2, September 22): 125–51.

Higham, John. 1956. "American Immigration Policy in Historical Perspective." *Law and Contemporary Problems* 21(2, Spring): 213–35. https://doi.org/10 .2307/1190500.

Hirschman, Charles. 2004. "The Origins and Demise of the Concept of Race." *Population and Development Review* 30(3, September): 385–415. https:// doi.org/10.1111/j.1728-4457.2004.00021.x.

———. 2013. "The Contributions of Immigrants to American Culture." *Daedalus* 142(3): 26–47.

Hirschman, Charles, and Douglas S. Massey. 2008. "Places and Peoples: The New American Mosaic." In *New Faces in New Places: The Changing Geography of American Immigration*, edited by Douglas S. Massey. New York: Russell Sage Foundation.

Hirschman, Charles, and Elizabeth Mogford. 2009. "Immigration and the American Industrial Revolution from 1880 to 1920." *Social Science Research* 38(4): 897–920.

Hochschild, Jennifer L., and John Mollenkopf. 2008. "The Complexities of Immigration: Why Western Countries Struggle with Immigration Politics and Policies." Migration Policy Institute. https://www.migrationpolicy.org /sites/default/files/publications/Hochschild-FINAL%5B1%5D.pdf.

Hope Church Adult Education. 2024. Presentation on YouTube, January 7, 2024. https://www.youtube.com/watch?v=jiBi_vIqzHg.

Huntington, Samuel P. 2004. "The Hispanic Challenge." *Foreign Policy* 141(March/April): 30–45. https://doi.org/10.2307/4147547.

Hutchinson, Edward P. 1956. *Immigrants and Their Children, 1850–1950.* New York: Wiley.

Isensee, Laura. 2015. "How a Dad Helped Start the Fight for Better Public School Funding in Texas." Houston Public Media, September 7. https://www.houstonpublicmedia.org/articles/news/2015/09/07/59720/how-a-dad-helped-start-the-fight-for-better-public-school-funding-in-texas-2/.

Jackson, Jacob. 2016. "Reducing Tuition Volatility at California's Universities." Public Policy Institute of California, April 28. https://www.ppic.org/blog/reducing-tuition-volatility-at-californias-universities/.

Jiménez, Tomás R. 2010. *Replenished Ethnicity: Mexican Americans, Immigration, and Identity.* Berkeley: University of California Press.

Jiménez, Tomás R., and David Fitzgerald. 2007. "Mexican Assimilation: A Temporal and Spatial Reorientation." *Du Bois Review* 4(2): 337–54. https://doi.org/10.1017/S1742058X07070191.

Jiménez, Tomás R., Julie Park, and Juan Pedroza. 2018. "The New Third Generation: Post-1965 Immigration and the Next Chapter in the Long Story of Assimilation." *International Migration Review* 52(4, December): 1040–79. https://doi.org/10.1111/imre.12343.

Kao, Grace, and Marta Tienda. 1995. "Optimism and Achievement: The Educational Performance of Immigrant Youth." *Social Science Quarterly* 76(1): 1–19.

Kaplan, Robert M., Zhengyi Fang, and James Kirby. 2017. "Educational Attainment and Health Outcomes: Data from the Medical Expenditures Panel Survey." *Health Psychology* 36(6, June): 598–608. https://doi.org/10.1037/hea0000431.

Kasarda, John D. 1989. "Urban Industrial Transition and the Underclass." *Annals of the American Academy of Political and Social Science* 501(1): 26–47. https://doi.org/10.1177/0002716289501001002.

Kasinitz, Philip, John H. Mollenkopf, Jennifer Holdaway, and Mary C. Waters. 2008. *Inheriting the City: The Children of Immigrants Come of Age.* Cambridge, Mass., and New York: Harvard University Press and Russell Sage Foundation.

Katz, Michael B. 1976. "The Origins of Public Education: A Reassessment." *History of Education Quarterly* 16(4, Winter): 381–407. https://doi.org/10.2307/367722.

Kibbe, Pauline R. 1946. *Latin Americans in Texas.* Albuquerque: University of New Mexico Press.

Kim, Dongbin, and John L. Rury. 2007. "The Changing Profile of College Access: The Truman Commission and Enrollment Patterns in the Postwar Era." *History of Education Quarterly* 47(3): 302–27.

Kim, Sukkoo. 2007. "Immigration, Industrial Revolution, and Urban Growth in the United States, 1820–1920: Factor Endowments, Technology and Geography." Working Paper 12900. Cambridge, Mass.: National Bureau of Economic Research, February.

Kratz, Jessie. 2021. "El Movimiento: The Chicano Movement and Hispanic Identity in the United States." National Archives, Pieces of History, September 23. https://prologue.blogs.archives.gov/2021/09/23/el-movimiento -the-chicano-movement-and-hispanic-identity-in-the-united-states/.

Lauen, Douglas Lee, and S. Michael Gaddis. 2012. "Shining a Light or Fumbling in the Dark? The Effects of NCLB's Subgroup-Specific Accountability on Student Achievement." *Educational Evaluation and Policy Analysis* 34(2): 185–208.

Lazarin, Melissa. 2022. "How State Assessments Became and Remain a Driver for Equity for English Learners." Migration Policy Institute, June 23. https://www.migrationpolicy.org/news/state-assessments-driver-equity -english-learners.

Lazerson, Marvin. 1977. "Understanding American Catholic Educational History." *History of Education Quarterly* 17(3, Autumn): 297–317. https:// doi.org/10.2307/367880.

Leach, Mark A., Jennifer Van Hook, and James D. Bachmeier. 2018. "Using Linked Data to Investigate True Intergenerational Change: Three Generations over Seven Decades." CARRA Working Paper Series. Washington: U.S. Bureau of the Census, Center for Administrative Records Research and Applications.

Lee, Jennifer, and Min Zhou. 2015. *The Asian American Achievement Paradox.* New York: Russell Sage Foundation.

Lee, Jongkwan, Giovanni Peri, and Vasil Yasenov. 2022. "The Labor Market Effects of Mexican Repatriations: Longitudinal Evidence from the 1930s." *Journal of Public Economics* 205(January): 104558.

Lieberson, Stanley. 1980. *A Piece of the Pie: Blacks and White Immigrants since 1880.* Berkeley: University of California Press.

Lleras-Muney, Adriana. 2002. "Were Compulsory Attendance and Child Labor Laws Effective? An Analysis from 1915 to 1939." *Journal of Law and Economics* 45(2, October): 401–35.

Lleras-Muney, Adriana, and Allison Shertzer. 2015. "Did the Americanization Movement Succeed? An Evaluation of the Effect of English-Only and Compulsory Schooling Laws on Immigrants." *American Economic Journal: Economic Policy* 7(3, August): 258–90. https://doi.org/10.1257/pol.2012 0219.

Logan, John R., and Brian J. Stults. 2021. "The Persistence of Segregation in the Metropolis: New Findings from the 2020 Census." Brown University, Diversity and Disparities Project. https://s4.ad.brown.edu/Projects /Diversity.

———. 2022. "Metropolitan Segregation: No Breakthrough in Sight." Washington: U.S. Bureau of the Census.

Logan, John R., Wenquan Zhang, and Richard D. Alba. 2002. "Immigrant Enclaves and Ethnic Communities in New York and Los Angeles." *American Sociological Review* 67(2, April): 299–322. https://doi.org/10.2307/308 8897.

Lopez, David E., and Ricardo D. Stanton-Salazar. 2001. "Mexican Americans: A Second Generation at Risk." In *Ethnicities: Children of Immigrants in America*, edited by Rubén G. Rumbaut and Alejandro Portes. Berkeley and New York: University of California Press and Russell Sage Foundation.

Louie, Vivian. 2012. *Keeping the Immigrant Bargain: The Costs and Rewards of Success in America.* New York: Russell Sage Foundation.

Lowrey, Kendal, and Jennifer Van Hook. 2021. "Standing on Their Own Two Feet: How the New Public Charge Rules Could Impact Non-European LPR Applicants." *Population Research and Policy Review* 41(March 31): 559–82. https://doi.org/10.1007/s11113-021-09648-5.

Lowrey, Kendal, Jennifer Van Hook, James D. Bachmeier, and Thomas Foster. 2021. "Leapfrogging the Melting Pot? European Immigrants' Intergenerational Mobility across the Twentieth Century." *Sociological Science* 8(December 17): 480–512. https://doi.org/10.15195/v8.a23.

Lu, Yao, Qian He, and Jeanne Brooks-Gunn. 2020. "Diverse Experience of Immigrant Children: How Do Separation and Reunification Shape Their Development?" *Child Development* 91(1, January/February): e146–63. https://doi.org/10.1111/cdev.13171.

Lynch, Scott M. 2003. "Cohort and Life-Course Patterns in the Relationship between Education and Health: A Hierarchical Approach." *Demography* 40(2): 309–31.

Magnuson, Katherine, Claudia Lahaie, and Jane Waldfogel. 2006. "Preschool and School Readiness of Children of Immigrants." *Social Science Quarterly* 87(5): 1241–62.

Martin, Rachel. 2019. "Rule Would Penalize Immigrants to U.S. for Needing Benefits." *Morning Edition*, NPR, August 13. https://www.npr.org/2019 /08/13/750727515/rule-would-penalize-immigrants-to-u-s-for-needing -benefits.

Massey, Catherine G., Katie R. Genadek, J. Trent Alexander, Todd K. Gardner, and Amy O'Hara. 2018. "Linking the 1940 U.S. Census with Modern Data." *Historical Methods* 51(4): 246–57.

Massey, Douglas S., Rafael Alarcón, Jorge Durand, and Humberto González. 1987. *Return to Aztlan: The Social Process of International Migration from Western Mexico.* Berkeley: University of California Press.

Massey, Douglas S., and Nancy A. Denton. 1993. *American Apartheid: Segregation and the Making of the Underclass.* Cambridge, Mass.: Harvard University Press.

Massey, Douglas S., Jorge Durand, and Nolan J. Malone. 2002. *Beyond Smoke and Mirrors: Mexican Immigration in an Era of Economic Integration.* New York: Russell Sage Foundation.

Massey, Douglas S., Jorge Durand, and Karen A. Pren. 2015. "Border Enforcement and Return Migration by Documented and Undocumented Mexicans." *Journal of Ethnic and Migration Studies* 41(7): 1015–40.

McLoyd, Vonnie C. 1998. "Socioeconomic Disadvantage and Child Development: American Psychologist." *American Psychologist: Applications of Developmental Science* 53(2, February): 185–204. https://doi.org/10.1037/0003-066X.53.2.185.

Menchaca, Martha. 1995. *The Mexican Outsiders: A Community History of Marginalization and Discrimination in California.* Austin: University of Texas Press.

Meyer, John W., David Tyack, Joane Nagel, and Audri Gordon. 1979. "Public Education as Nation-Building in America: Enrollments and Bureaucratization in the American States, 1870–1930." *American Journal of Sociology* 85(3): 591–613.

Meyer, Stephen. 1980. "Adapting the Immigrant to the Line: Americanization in the Ford Factory, 1914–1921." *Journal of Social History* 14(1, Fall). https://doi.org/10.1353/jsh/14.1.67.

Mintz, John. 2000. "George W. Bush: The Record in Texas." *Washington Post*, April 20. https://www.washingtonpost.com/archive/politics/2000/04/21/george-w-bush-the-record-in-texas/3fcc6109-7332-45a6-9658-de52abc4c4ed/.

Mirowsky, John, and Catherine E. Ross. 2003. *Education, Social Status, and Health.* New York: Routledge.

Mitchell, Anaïs. 2010. "Why We Build the Wall." From *Hadestown* (album). Buffalo, N.Y.: Righteous Babe Records.

———. 2016. "Why We Build the Wall." *HuffPost Entertainment*, November 4. https://www.huffpost.com/entry/why-we-build-the-wall_b_581cbcb7e4b044f827a78c0a.

Montejano, David. 1987. *Anglos and Mexicans in the Making of Texas, 1836–1986.* Austin: University of Texas Press.

Montez, Jennifer Karas, Robert A. Hummer, and Mark D. Hayward. 2012. "Educational Attainment and Adult Mortality in the United States: A Systematic Analysis of Functional Form." *Demography* 49(1, February 1): 315–36. https://doi.org/10.1007/s13524-011-0082-8.

Moore, Joan, and Raquel Pinderhughes. 1993. "Introduction." In *In the Barrios: Latinos and the Underclass Debate*, edited by Joan Moore and Raquel Pinderhughes. New York: Russell Sage Foundation.

Moore, R. Laurence. 1986. *Religious Outsiders and the Making of Americans.* New York: Oxford University Press.

Myers, Dowell. 2007. *Immigrants and Boomers: Forging a New Social Contract for the Future of America.* New York: Russell Sage Foundation.

National Academies of Sciences, Engineering, and Medicine. 2015. *The Integration of Immigrants into American Society*, edited by Mary C. Waters and Marisa Gerstein Pineau. Washington, D.C.: National Academies Press.

National Immigration Law Center. 2023. "Basic Facts about In-State Tuition." Updated August 2023. https://www.nilc.org/issues/education/basic-facts -instate/.

National Opinion Research Center. 2020. "National Opinion Research Center General Social Survey 1972–2021." Ithaca, N.Y.: Roper Center for Public Opinion Research, Cornell University. https://doi.org/10.25940/ROPER -31118778.

Ngai, Mae M. 2004. *Impossible Subjects: Illegal Aliens and the Making of Modern America*. Princeton, N.J.: Princeton University Press.

———. 2006. "Birthright Citizenship and the Alien Citizen." *Fordham Law Review* 75: 2521.

Noori Farzan, Antonia. 2019. "Tom Brokaw Apologizes after Saying 'Hispanics Should Work Harder at Assimilation.'" *Washington Post*, January 28. https://www.washingtonpost.com/nation/2019/01/28/tom-brokaw -apologizes-after-saying-hispanics-should-work-harder-assimilation/.

Ogbu, John U. 1987. "Variability in Minority School Performance: A Problem in Search of an Explanation." *Anthropology and Education Quarterly* 18(4): 312–34.

Olneck, Michael R. 1989. "Americanization and the Education of Immigrants, 1900–1925: An Analysis of Symbolic Action." *American Journal of Education* 97(4): 398–423.

Park, Julie, and Dowell Myers. 2010. "Intergenerational Mobility in the Post-1965 Immigration Era: Estimates by an Immigrant Generation Cohort Method." *Demography* 47(2, May 1): 369–92. https://doi.org/10.1353 /dem.0.0105.

Parker, Christopher Sebastian. 2021. "Status Threat: Moving the Right Further to the Right?" *Daedalus* 150(2, Spring): 56–75. https://doi.org/10.1162 /daed_a_01846.

Passel, Jeffrey S. 2005. "Rise, Peak, and Decline: Trends in U.S. Immigration 1992–2004." Pew Research Center, September 27. https://www.pewresearch .org/hispanic/2005/09/27/rise-peak-and-decline-trends-in-us-immi gration-1992-2004/.

Passel, Jeffrey S., and D'Vera Cohn. 2009. "Mexican Immigrants: How Many Come? How Many Leave?" Washington, D.C.: Pew Hispanic Center, July 22. https://www.pewresearch.org/hispanic/2009/07/22/mexican-immigrants -how-many-come-how-many-leave/.

———. 2017. "Immigration Projected to Drive Growth in U.S. Working-Age Population through at Least 2035." Pew Research Center, March 8. https:// www.pewresearch.org/short-reads/2017/03/08/immigration-projected-to -drive-growth-in-u-s-working-age-population-through-at-least-2035/.

Perlmann, Joel. 1988. *Ethnic Differences: Schooling and Social Structure among the Irish, Italians, Jews, and Blacks in an American City, 1880–1935*. Cambridge: Cambridge University Press.

———. 2005. *Italians Then, Mexicans Now: Immigrant Origins and the Second-Generation Progress, 1890–2000.* New York: Russell Sage Foundation.

Pew Research Center. 2018a. "Shifting Public Views on Legal Immigration into the U.S." June. https://www.pewresearch.org/politics/2018/06/28/shifting-public-views-on-legal-immigration-into-the-u-s/.

———. 2018b. "The Generation Gap in American Politics." March. https://www.pewresearch.org/politics/2018/03/01/the-generation-gap-in-american-politics/.

Pierce, Webster H. 1931. *Ninety-First Report of the Superintendent of Public Instruction of the State of Michigan for the Biennium 1929–1931.* Lansing: State of Michigan, Department of Public Instruction.

Portes, Alejandro, and Rubén G. Rumbaut. 2001. *Legacies: The Story of the Immigrant Second Generation.* Berkeley: University of California Press.

———. 2014. *Immigrant America: A Portrait,* 4th ed. Berkeley: University of California Press.

Portes, Alejandro, and Min Zhou. 1993. "The New Second Generation: Segmented Assimilation and Its Variants." *Annals of the American Academy of Political and Social Science* 530(1): 74–96.

Progressive National Committee. 1912. "A Contract with the People: Platform of the Progressive Party Adopted at Its First National Convention." New York: Progressive National Committee.

Putnam, Robert D. 2007. "E Pluribus Unum: Diversity and Community in the Twenty-First Century: The 2006 Johan Skytte Prize Lecture." *Scandinavian Political Studies* 30(2, June): 137–74. https://doi.org/10.1111/j.1467-9477.2007.00176.x.

Radde, Kaitlyn. 2023. "Child Labor Violations Are on the Rise as Some States Look to Loosen Their Rules." NPR, February 26. https://www.npr.org/2023/02/26/1157368469/child-labor-violations-increase-states-loosen-rules.

Reyes, Belinda I. 2001. "Immigrant Trip Duration: The Case of Immigrants from Western Mexico." *International Migration Review* 35(4): 1185–1204.

———. 2004. "Changes in Trip Duration for Mexican Immigrants to the United States." *Population Research and Policy Review* 23: 235–57.

Richardson, John G. 1980. "Variation in Date of Enactment of Compulsory School Attendance Laws: An Empirical Inquiry." *Sociology of Education* 53(3, July): 153–63. https://doi.org/10.2307/2112410.

———. 1984. "The American States and the Age of School Systems." *American Journal of Education* 92(4): 473–502.

Riis, Jacob A. 1890. *How the Other Half Lives: Studies among the Tenements of New York.* New York: Charles Scribner's Sons.

Ro, Annie, Tim A. Bruckner, Michael Pham Huynh, Senxi Du, and Andrew Young. 2023. "Emergency Department Utilization among Undocumented Latino Patients during the COVID-19 Pandemic." *Journal of Racial and*

Ethnic Health Disparities 10(4): 2020–27. https://doi.org/10.1007/s40615
-022-01382-8.

Rosenblum, Marc R., William A. Kandel, Clare Ribando Seelke, and Ruth Ellen Wasem. 2012. "Mexican Migration to the United States: Policy and Trends." Washington: Congressional Research Service.

Rothstein, Richard. 2017. *The Color of Law: The Forgotten History of How Our Government Segregated America.* New York: Liveright.

Ruggles, Steven, Sarah Flood, Matthew Sobek, Daniel Backman, Annie Chen, Grace Cooper, Stephanie Richards, Renae Rodgers, and Megan Shouweiler. 2024. "IPUMS USA: Version 15.0 [Dataset]." Minneapolis: IPUMS. https://doi.org/10.18128/D010.V15.0.

Sanchez, George I. 1932. "Group Differences and Spanish-Speaking Children—A Critical Review." *Journal of Applied Psychology* 16(5): 549.

Sanchez, George J. 1993. *Becoming Mexican American: Ethnicity, Culture, and Identity in Chicano Los Angeles, 1900–1945.* New York: Oxford University Press.

Southern Education Foundation. 2009. "No Time to Lose: Why America Needs an Education Amendment to the U.S. Constitution to Improve Public Education." https://southerneducation.org/wp-content/uploads/documents/no-time-to-lose.pdf.

Springer, Matthew G. 2008. "The Influence of an NCLB Accountability Plan on the Distribution of Student Test Score Gains." *Economics of Education Review* 27(5, October): 556–63. https://doi.org/10.1016/j.econedurev.2007.06.004.

State of California. 1924. Thirty-First Biennial Report of the Superintendent of Public Instruction. Sacramento: California Department of Education.

State of Texas. 1924. The Twenty-Third Biennial Report. Austin, Tex.: State Department of Education.

Steinberg, Stephen. 1981. *The Ethnic Myth: Race, Ethnicity, and Class in America.* Boston: Beacon Press.

Sugrue, Thomas J. 2005. *The Origins of the Urban Crisis: Race and Inequality in Postwar Detroit.* Princeton, N.J.: Princeton University Press. (Originally published in 1996.)

Suhay, Elizabeth, Mark Tenenbaum, and Austin Bartola. 2022. "Explanations for Inequality and Partisan Polarization in the U.S., 1980–2020." *The Forum* 20(1, August 5): 5–36. https://doi.org/10.1515/for-2022-2052.

Taylor, Paul S. 1930. *Mexican Labor in the United States: Dimmit County, Winter Garden District, South Texas,* vol. 1, no. 5. Berkeley: University of California Publications in Economics.

———. 1934. *An American-Mexican Frontier: Nueces County, Texas.* Chapel Hill: University of North Carolina Press.

Telles, Edward E., and Vilma Ortiz. 2009. *Generations of Exclusion: Mexican Americans, Assimilation, and Race.* New York: Russell Sage Foundation.

Tesch, Noah, and Editors of Encyclopaedia Britannica. 2014. "Fair Employment Practices Committee: United States History." Britannica, March 14, 2014. https://www.britannica.com/topic/Fair-Employment-Practices-Committee.

Texas Education Agency. 2000. *2000 Comprehensive Biennial Report on Texas Public Schools: A Report to the 77th Texas Legislature.* https://tea.texas.gov/sites/default/files/Comp_Annual_Biennial_2000.pdf.

Tobin, Maurice J., and Ewan Clague. 1949. "Consumers' Prices in the United States 1942–1948: Analysis of Changes in Cost of Living." *Bulletin of the United States Bureau of Labor Statistics* 966.

Tyack, David. 1976. "Ways of Seeing: An Essay on the History of Compulsory Schooling." *Harvard Educational Review* 46(3, September 1): 355–89. https://doi.org/10.17763/haer.46.3.v73405527200106v.

U.S. Bureau of the Census. 2023. "U.S. Population Projected to Begin Declining in Second Half of Century." U.S. Bureau of the Census, November 9. https://www.census.gov/newsroom/press-releases/2023/population-projections.html.

U.S. Commission on Civil Rights. 1965. *The Voting Rights Act: The First Months.* Washington: U.S. Commission on Civil Rights. https://lccn.loc.gov/66060144.

———. 2001. "Voting Rights and Political Representation in the Mississippi Delta." In *Racial and Ethnic Tensions in American Communities: Poverty, Inequality, and Discrimination*, vol. 7, *The Mississippi Delta Report*. Washington: U.S. Commission on Civil Rights. https://www.usccr.gov/files/pubs/msdelta/ch3.htm.

U.S. Department of Education. 2023. "Common Core of Data (CCD)." Washington: National Center for Health Statistics.

———. n.d. "Every Student Succeeds Act (ESSA)." https://www.ed.gov/essa?src=rn.

U.S. Government. 1964. "Civil Rights Act of 1964." Enrolled Acts and Resolutions of Congress, 1789–2011, July 2, 1964. General Records of the U.S. Government, record group 11. Washington: National Archives.

U.S. Office of Immigration Statistics. 2022. "Yearbook of Immigration Statistics, 2022." Washington: U.S. Department of Homeland Security. https://www.dhs.gov/ohss/topics/immigration/yearbook/2022.

U.S. Office of the Interior. 1928. *Biennial Survey of Education*, vol. 1. Washington: U.S. Government Printing Office and U.S. Department of Education.

Valdes, Marcela. 2023. "Why Can't We Stop Unauthorized Immigration? Because It Works." *New York Times Magazine*, October 1. https://www.nytimes.com/2023/10/01/magazine/economy-illegal-immigration.html.

Van Hook, Jennifer, and Frank D. Bean. 2009. "Immigrant Welfare Receipt: Implications for Immigrant Settlement and Integration." In *Immigrants and*

Welfare: The Impact of Welfare Reform on America's Newcomers, edited by Michael Fix. New York: Russell Sage Foundation.

Van Hook, Jennifer, Julia Gelatt, and Ariel G. Ruiz Soto. 2023. "A Turning Point for the Unauthorized Immigrant Population in the United States." Migration Policy Institute, September 13. https://www.migrationpolicy .org/news/turning-point-us-unauthorized-immigrant-population.

Vega, Lilia. 2014. "The History of UC Tuition since 1868." *The Daily Californian*, December 22. https://dailycal.org/2014/12/22/history-uc-tuition -since-1868.

Vollmer, Sebastian, Christian Bommer, Aditi Krishna, Kenneth Harttgen, and S. V. Subramanian. 2017. "The Association of Parental Education with Childhood Undernutrition in Low- and Middle-Income Countries: Comparing the Role of Paternal and Maternal Education." *International Journal of Epidemiology* 46(1, February): 312–23. https://doi.org/10.1093/ije /dyw133.

Wagner, Deborah, and Mary Layne. 2014. "The Person Identification Validation System (PVS): Applying the Center for Administrative Records Research and Applications' (CARRA) Record Linkage Software." CARRA Working Paper Series. Washington: U.S. Bureau of the Census.

Waldinger, Roger, and Cynthia Feliciano. 2004. "Will the New Second Generation Experience 'Downward Assimilation'? Segmented Assimilation Re-Assessed." *Ethnic and Racial Studies* 27(3, May 1): 376–402. https://doi.org /10.1080/01491987042000189196.

Waters, Mary C. 1990. *Ethnic Options: Choosing Identities in America.* Berkeley: University of California Press.

Waters, Mary C., and Tomás R. Jiménez. 2005. "Assessing Immigrant Assimilation: New Empirical and Theoretical Challenges." *Annual Review of Sociology* 31(1, August 1): 105–25. https://doi.org/10.1146/annurev.soc.29 .010202.100026.

Waters, Mary C., Reed Ueda, and Helen B. Marrow. 2007. *The New Americans: A Guide to Immigration since 1965.* Cambridge, Mass.: Harvard University Press.

WETA Washington, D.C., and Ark Media. 2015. *The Italian Americans* (documentary). PBS. https://www.pbs.org/show/italian-americans/.

White, Michael J., and Erica Jade Mullen. 2016. "Socioeconomic Attainment in the Ellis Island Era." *Social Science History* 40(1): 147–81. https://doi .org/10.1017/ssh.2015.84.

Wilson, William Julius. 1978. *The Declining Significance of Race: Blacks and Changing American Institutions.* Chicago: University of Chicago Press.

———. 1987. *The Truly Disadvantaged: The Inner City, the Underclass, and Public Policy.* Chicago: University of Chicago Press.

Wojtkiewicz, Roger A., and Katharine M. Donato. 1995. "Hispanic Educational Attainment: The Effects of Family Background and Nativity." *Social Forces* 74(2): 559–74.

Yoshikawa, Hirokazu. 2011. *Immigrants Raising Citizens: Undocumented Parents and Their Children.* New York: Russell Sage Foundation.

Yoshikawa, Hirokazu, and Ariel Kalil. 2011. "The Effects of Parental Undocumented Status on the Developmental Contexts of Young Children in Immigrant Families: Undocumented Status in Immigrant Families." *Child Development Perspectives* 5(4, December): 291–97. https://doi.org/10.1111/j.1750-8606.2011.00204.x.

Zsembik, Barbara A., and Daniel Llanes. 1996. "Generational Differences in Educational Attainment among Mexican Americans." *Social Science Quarterly* 77(2): 363–74.

~ Index ~

Tables and figures are listed in **boldface**.

racism: assimilation and, 21; Civil
Rights Era and, 19–20; early-vintage
Mexican Americans and, 59, 64–71,
71, 78–83, **80**, **82**; ethnocentrism
vs., 25; Jim Crow laws, 15, 26, 65,
87–90, 95, 126; public school expan-
sion and, 87–92, **89**, **91**; racial hier-
archies and, 38, 43–44, 57, 68–69,
79; segregation and, 65, 101–4, **103**,
120; structural, 78–83, **80**, **82**, 86,
90, 98, 119–20, 126
RAISE (Reforming American Immigra-
tion for Strong Employment) Act
(2017, proposed), 118
Remaking the American Mainstream
(Alba & Nee), 22
Richards, Ann, 109
Richardson, Friend, 70
Richardson, John G., 88
Riis, Jacob, 41
Rodriguez, Demitrio, 106–7
Rodriguez, Jonny, 127
Roosevelt, Theodore, 41

San Antonio ISD v. Rodriguez (1973),
106–7
Sanchez, George, 61, 62, 63, 69
segmented assimilation theory, 23, 26,
43, 45
SFFA v. Harvard (2023), 124–25
SFFA v. UNC (2023), 124–25
Shertzer, Allison, 52
social cohesion, 9, 15, 54, 57
social Darwinism, 44–45, 64
social status hierarchy, 41, 50–51, 57
Southern United States: English language school funding in, 70, **71**;
public school funding in, 87–92, **89**,
91. *See also* Texas
status attainment paradigm, 43
stereotypes, 44, 52, 56, 101, 117, 118
Streets of Gold (Abramitzky & Boustan),
12, 132*n*30
Supreme Court, U.S.: on bilingual education, 109; on civil rights laws including Hispanics, 100; on constitutional right to education, 106–7; on
desegregation of public schools, 100,

101; on education for undocumented
immigrants, 121; on race-based affirmative action in college admissions,
124–25

Taylor, Paul, 66, 85
Telles, Edward, 13
Texas: agricultural and manufacturing
industry in, 61, 67–68, 99; denying
education to Mexican children, 68,
70, 85, 86–87, 90; Industrial Era immigrants as source of labor in, 15;
lack of opportunities for immigrants
in, 9; Mexican–American War and,
60, 66, 100; public school funding
in, 92, 95, 104–7, **105**, **108**,
136*n*33; public school reforms in,
109–10; segregation of public schools
in, 101–4, **103**; structural racism in,
67, 78–83, **80**, **82**, 126
third-generation delay: bias in study of,
11, 28, 31, 125; in educational assimilation, 11–12, 14–15, 26–31,
27; place and time dependence, 125;
structural racism and, 120; vintage
heterogeneity and, 28–31, **29**–**30**
Tienda, Marta, 55
Treaty of Guadalupe Hidalgo (1849),
60, 66, 100
Trejo, Stephen J., 27–28, **27**
Trump, Donald, 100–101, 116, 118–19

unauthorized immigration. *See* undocumented immigrants
undocumented immigrants: assimilation, barriers to, 120; Bracero Program, end of, 120–21; deportations
of welfare users, 118; employment
and, 12, 121–23; Great Depression
and, 63–64; kinship networks and
residential segregation, 103–4; migration rates of, 121–23; negative depic-
tions of, 117; parent deportations
and child welfare, 121–22; social
movements for, 100–101
U.S. Census Bureau data: Current Population Survey, 1, 27–28, 32, 131*n*37;
on demographic changes, 117; on

U.S. Census Bureau data (*cont.*)
early-vintage Mexican Americans,
66–67; on education in California vs.
Texas, 70, 135*n*48; ethnic attrition
and, 31–32, 46; following generations through, 12, 13–14; identifying
persons of Mexican origins through,
135*n*48; on increase of Mexican-born
individuals in early 1900s, 60–61,
63; on location-based educational attainment, 33, 81, 131*n*37; review
board, 32. *See also* IGENS-20 data
U.S. Department of Education, 36

Valdes, Marcela, 122
Vallejo, Jody, 103
Vento, Joey, 8–9
vintage heterogeneity, 15, 20, 28–31,
29–30, 38, 130–31*n*29
vocational training, 51, 70, 124. *See also*
post-secondary education
voting rights, 65, 100
Voting Rights Act (1965), 100

Western United States: English language
school funding in, 70, **71**; public

school funding in, 87–92, **89**, **91**. *See
also* California
White, Michael, 54
whites: black-white binary, challenges to,
65; as comparison group, 37; current
educational attainment levels of,
132*n*40; demographic changes and,
117; early-vintage Mexican Americans compared, 72–74, **73**; educational attainment of Industrial Era
citizens, 46–49, **47**, 53; European Industrial Era immigrants classified as,
64, 65; family immigration stories of,
1–8; Mexican Americans classified as,
66–67, 69, 100; middle-vintage Mexican Americans compared, 81–83,
82; parental status and educational
attainment, 74–78, **75–77**; racialization of Jewish and Italian immigrants, 44–45; third-generation education attainment, **27**, 27–28. *See
also* Americanization movement; discrimination; ethnocentrism; racism
Wilson, William Julius, 23

Zhou, Min, 12, 23, 55